NOBODY
EVER
ASKED
BEFORE

A Parable About Empowerment, Inclusion, and Sustainable Transformation

John Rizzo

Published by MoffittPress, Inc., Syracuse NY. Published simultaneously in Canada. No part of this publication may be reproduced, stored in a retrieval system, or transmitted in any form or by any means, electronic, mechanical, photocopying, recording, scanning, or otherwise, except as permitted under Section 107 or 108 of the 1976 United States Copyright Act, without the prior written permission of the Publisher. Requests to the Publisher for permission should be addressed to MoffittPress, Inc. johnarizzo1@icloud.com.

Special requests should be directed to john.rizzo@moffittxl.com.

Library of Congress Cataloging-in-Publication Data is Available:
ISBN 979-8-9953977-0-0 (Paperback)
ISBN 979-8-9953977-1-7 (Hardcover)
ISBN 979-8-9953977-2-4 (EPUB)

DEDICATION

To all the workers whose intelligence was ignored but never extinguished.

To all the managers who chose to listen.

To all the organizations brave enough to change.

And to everyone who believes that work can be a source of dignity, not just income.

CONTENTS

ACKNOWLEDGMENTS

This book would not exist without the workers who taught me that wisdom lives on every factory floor, in every warehouse, in every office, in every place where people do real work with their hands and minds. To all of you who shared your insights, your frustrations, and your dreams, thank you for trusting me with your stories.

I owe an immeasurable debt to Bill Moffitt, whose mentorship shaped not only my understanding of organizations but my understanding of what it means to truly listen. His influence echoes through every page of this novel, and through every workshop I have ever facilitated.

To my colleagues at Talus and MoffittXL, past and present, who have helped refine these ideas through countless conversations, debates, and real-world applications, your partnership has made this work possible.

To the leaders who took risks, who chose to trust their workers, who believed that there had to be a better way, you proved that transformation is possible. Your courage gives me hope for the future of American business.

To my family, who endured my absences and my obsessions, who listened to me talk about Mary Parker Follett and the Hawthorne experiments far more than any family should have to, your patience and love sustained me.

The ideas in this novel draw on the work of Mary Parker Follett, Elton Mayo, Douglas McGregor, Chris Argyris, W. Edwards Deming, Taiichi Ohno, and countless other thinkers who understood that organizations are human systems, and that lasting change requires treating people with dignity and respect.

NOBODY
EVER
ASKED
BEFORE

PREFACE

"The people doing the work already know how to make it better."

— *Creating Value,* (Wiley, 2025)

This is a multi-generational business novel tracing the history of participative management from the 1927 Hawthorne experiments to a contemporary factory transformation in Syracuse, NY. The narrative demonstrates how worker intelligence, when respected and applied, can transform failing organizations into models of sustainable success. The characters, companies, and specific events described in these pages are based on my own experiences. The ideas behind them are real, grounded in nearly a century of management research and three decades of my own experience helping organizations transform.

The story begins, as so many stories do, with a simple observation that refused to let me go.

Early in my career, I moved a machine six inches because a worker asked. It was a small adjustment, made possible only because someone finally thought to listen to what would make his job easier. That six-inch move eliminated hours of wasted motion every week. It improved quality. It reduced injuries. And it revealed something that should have been obvious but wasn't: the people who do the work understand the work better than anyone else.

Why hadn't anyone asked before?

This question led me to Mary Parker Follett, a management theorist who died in 1933 but whose ideas feel more relevant today than ever. It led me to the Hawthorne experiments, where researchers discovered that simply paying attention to workers, asking their opinions, treating them as thinking human beings, could transform productivity in ways that no physical improvement could match. It led me to study how American ideas about participative management traveled to Japan, were refined and systematized, and then returned to America as a 'miracle' that was really wisdom coming home.

This novel attempts to make those ideas visceral and human. The theoretical frameworks are accurate. You can find them in any good management textbook. But theory alone doesn't change organizations.

Stories do. Relationships do. The daily, patient work of treating people with respect does.

I've tried to create characters who feel real because they're based on real people I've known, workers whose intelligence was wasted for decades, managers who learned to listen, and leaders who found the courage to trust their people. The transformation at Meridian Manufacturing mirrors many of my own experiences and counseling from my mentor. The principles are based on my book, ***Creating Value: Empowering People for Sustainable Success***, (Wiley, 2025).

The failure rate of organizational change initiatives is notoriously high, with some estimates suggesting that 70% of transformation efforts fail to achieve their intended goals. This novel asks why. And it suggests an answer that should be obvious but somehow isn't: most change efforts fail because they don't genuinely engage the people who have to make them work.

The Afterword reflects on artificial intelligence and the future of empowerment. AI is transforming how work gets done. Some fear it will finally achieve Frederick Taylor's century-old dream, eliminating human judgment from work entirely. I believe the opposite. AI will not replace worker intelligence; it will amplify it. It is the suggestion box that never closes, the listener that never tires. AI can ensure that no insight is lost, no voice unheard.

The future of work is not artificial intelligence versus human intelligence. It is artificial intelligence in service of human intelligence, amplifying the voices that have been silenced for too long, ensuring that improvements never stop coming, never stop being heard, never stop being implemented.

If this story helps even one leader see their associates differently, helps even one organization tap the wisdom that exists on its front lines, helps even one worker feel heard and valued, then it will have accomplished its purpose.

PROLOGUE

The Foundations of Participative Management - Chicago, 1927

"Leadership is not defined by the exercise of power but by the capacity to increase the sense of power among those led. The most essential work of the leader is to create more leaders."

— Mary Parker Follett

The morning had begun with fog rolling off Lake Michigan, shrouding the industrial district in a gray embrace that seemed appropriate for what Mary Follett would later describe as "the most significant day of my intellectual life." She had taken a cab from the Palmer House, watching through rain-streaked windows as the city gradually revealed itself, first the elegant storefronts of the Loop, then the increasingly utilitarian architecture as they moved west toward Cicero.

The Hawthorne Works was a city unto itself, she realized as they approached. Fifty buildings spread across two hundred acres, employing more than forty thousand workers at its peak. The Western Electric Company had built not just a factory but a complete industrial ecosystem, power plants, fire stations, a hospital, recreation facilities, even a restaurant that served ten thousand meals daily. It was, in many ways, Frederick Taylor's dream made manifest: scientific management applied at scale, efficiency elevated to religion.

But something had happened here that Taylor's principles couldn't explain. Something that had brought Follett across the country despite her failing health, something that had sparked debates in academic circles from Harvard to Oxford. The Hawthorne experiments had begun as a simple study of workplace lighting and had evolved into something far more profound, a fundamental challenge to everything American industry believed about workers and productivity.

Follett had followed the experiments from their beginning in 1924, when the National Research Council had partnered with Western Electric to study the relationship between illumination and output. The hypothesis was straightforward: better lighting should improve productivity. But the results had defied explanation. When researchers increased the light, productivity rose. When they decreased it, productivity rose.

When they provided no additional light at all, productivity still rose.

The researchers had been baffled. They had controlled for every physical variable they could imagine, temperature, humidity, noise, rest periods, and still couldn't explain what was happening. It was as if the laws of cause and effect had been suspended within the walls of the relay assembly test room.

Elton Mayo had been brought in two years later to solve the puzzle. A professor of industrial research at Harvard, he approached the problem with the tools of psychology rather than engineering. And what he found would change the course of management theory forever, though Follett suspected even Mayo didn't fully understand the implications of his own discovery.

The cab pulled to a stop at Gate 4, and Follett gathered her things with the careful movements of someone who had learned to conserve energy. Her heart, weakened by years of overwork and the strain of constant travel, protested even this minor exertion. But she had not come this far to be stopped by physical limitations.

"Western Electric, ma'am?" the driver asked, perhaps noting her hesitation.

"Yes. The relay assembly test room."

"Ah, the experiment." The driver nodded with the knowing look of a local who had heard stories.

"My wife's cousin works in Building 15. Says they're doing strange things over there. Asking workers what they think, like it matters."

"It does matter," Follett said quietly, paying the fare. "It matters more than anyone yet understands." She stepped out into the industrial landscape, the noise and smell of manufacturing surrounding her like a familiar embrace. This was her world, the world of work, of production, of human beings organized to create value together. She had spent her life trying to understand it, to improve it, to help workers and managers alike see that their interests were not opposed but intertwined.

Today, perhaps, she would see proof that her ideas were more than academic theory.

• • •

The relay assembly test room occupied a corner of the third floor, its tall windows overlooking Cicero Avenue where the morning shift streamed through the gates. Mary stood perfectly still, her gray wool dress as severe as her expression, watching six women bend over their workbenches. Their fingers moved with practiced precision, selecting tiny springs, armatures, and insulators, assembling telephone relays with a speed that seemed almost mechanical.

But Follett knew better than to see only the mechanical.

"Remarkable, isn't it?" Dr. Elton Mayo spoke softly beside her, his Australian accent lending a curious formality to his enthusiasm. At forty-seven, Mayo cut an impressive figure, tall, lean, with the kind of carefully groomed mustache that suggested European sophistication. "We've been observing them for three years now."

"And what have you concluded?" Follett asked, though she suspected she already knew. She had come to Chicago specifically to see Mayo's experiments. At sixty, she had little patience for conventional wisdom, medical or otherwise.

Mayo consulted his clipboard, pages dense with data. "Initially, we hypothesized that improved lighting would increase productivity. So, we increased the illumination. Output went up. Then we decreased it. Output still went up. We've varied their rest periods, their work hours, even eliminated their breaks entirely."

He looked up, his eyes bright with discovery. "Production continues to increase regardless of the physical conditions."

One of the workers, a young woman with dark hair pinned back, glanced up from her work. Her eyes met Follett's for just a moment, sharp, intelligent eyes that seemed to hold a question. The nameplate on her workstation read "A. Kowalski."

"May I?" Follett moved toward the workstation before Mayo could object. She had never been one to observe from a distance.

Anna Kowalski's hands never stopped moving as Follett approached.

Spring, coil, armature, insulator, each piece finding its place in a rhythm perfected over thousands of repetitions.

"How long have you worked here, Miss Kowalski?" Anna's fingers paused for the briefest moment.

"Seven years, ma'am. Since I was sixteen."

"And before Dr. Mayo's experiments began?"

"Five years before that, ma'am."

Follett noticed the other women listening while pretending to work. The test room had developed its own social system, she realized, distinct from the factory floor beyond the partition.

"Tell me," Follett said, "what's different now? Not the lighting or the breaks, what's truly different?" Anna looked directly at her then, and Follett saw something shift in the young woman's expression, a recognition, perhaps, that here was someone asking a real question, not gathering data for a chart.

"They ask us things," Anna said simply. "Mr. Pennock, Dr. Mayo, the observers. They ask what we think about the work, about the changes. They write it down."

She gestured to the observer in the corner, a young man with a notebook who had been recording their conversation.

"Nobody ever asked before. Nobody ever wrote it down like it mattered."

The other women had stopped pretending to work now. A woman named Theresa added, "And when we said the chairs hurt our backs, they got new chairs. When we said the noon break was too late, they moved it earlier."

"Small things," another worker said.

"No," Follett corrected gently. "Not small at all."

Mayo had joined them, standing slightly apart, observing the observer being observed. "We call it the interview program," he explained.

"Twenty thousand workers interviewed so far. We listen to their complaints, their suggestions, their wisdom." "You listen to their wisdom," Follett interrupted.

That evening, in her room at the Palmer House, Follett opened her leather journal, the one she had carried since her days at Radcliffe.

The lamp cast a pool of yellow light on the page as she wrote: October 15, 1927. Today I witnessed the future of American industry, though I fear few will recognize it as such. In the relay assembly test room at Hawthorne, I saw what happens when we stop treating workers as mere extensions of machinery and begin treating them as thinking beings.

The productivity increases that Mayo measures are not the true revolution.

The revolution is in young Anna Kowalski's eyes when she realizes someone values her thoughts. It is in the observer's notebook that records not just motions and outputs but opinions and ideas.

For decades, I have argued for "power-with" rather than "power-over", for integration rather than domination. Today I saw it happening, almost by accident, in a corner of a

Chicago factory. Mayo believes he is studying the effects of working conditions on productivity. What he is actually studying is the effect of human dignity on human potential.

But I am troubled by a question: How long will it take for industry to truly understand this lesson? How many Annas labor in silence, their wisdom untapped, their voices unheard? I think of Frederick Taylor's time studies, his reduction of workers to mere motion, and I wonder if Mayo realizes he has begun to undo that damage.

I am sixty years old. My heart, the doctors tell me, is weakening. I will not live to see the full flowering of these ideas. But tonight, I allow myself to hope that somewhere, someday, a factory will recognize this truth fully: that every worker has a mind as well as hands, that wisdom exists at every level of an organization, and that the future belongs to those who learn to listen.

The young woman's words echo: "Nobody ever asked before." Such a simple revolution. Such a profound transformation. All beginning with the radical act of asking.

She set down her pen and looked out at the Chicago skyline, the electric lights spreading like stars across the darkness. Somewhere out there, Anna Kowalski was probably home now, perhaps telling her family about the strange woman who had asked different questions than the researchers.

Follett closed her journal, knowing she had witnessed something momentous. She could not know that Anna would name her daughter Catherine, who would name her son Stefan, who would name his son Tommy, each generation carrying forward the memory of being heard, the hunger to be valued, the wisdom waiting to be shared.

She could not know that her words would influence a young professor named Douglas McGregor, who would teach a student named Will Moffitt, who would mentor a young man named John Valerio, who would one day stand in another factory, listening to another worker named Kowalski.

All she knew, as she prepared for sleep in that Chicago hotel room, was that she had seen the future. It looked like Anna Kowalski being asked her opinion. It looked like someone writing down the answer as if it mattered.

Because it did matter. It would always matter.

The revolution had already begun.

LESSONS LEARNED

Mary Parker Follett's 'Power-With' Philosophy

In 1924, Mary Parker Follett articulated a distinction that would take industry nearly a century to embrace: the difference between 'power-over' (domination) and 'power-with' (collaboration). Follett argued that sustainable organizational success comes not from controlling workers but from integrating their knowledge and capabilities into decision-making. The scene at Hawthorne dramatizes the moment when American industry first glimpsed this truth, when Elton Mayo's researchers discovered that the simple act of asking workers their opinions produced results no physical improvement could match.

The Hawthorne Effect: Why Attention Matters

The Hawthorne experiments (1924-1932) revealed what Follett had intuited: workers respond to being valued as thinking human beings. When researchers paid attention to workers, asked their opinions, and treated their feedback as worthy of recording, productivity increased regardless of physical conditions. This phenomenon, now called the 'Hawthorne Effect,' demonstrates that human motivation is driven less by material conditions than by recognition and respect.

Creating Value Connection

In *Creating Value*, (Wiley, 2025), Rizzo argues that sustainable organizational success requires investing in people rather than treating them as costs to be minimized. Anna Kowalski's observation, 'Nobody ever asked before,' captures the tragedy of organizations that possess enormous, untapped intelligence and fail to access it simply because they never think to ask.

PART ONE: THE INHERITANCE
1990-1993

CHAPTER 1

The Inheritance of Organizational Wisdom - Syracuse Winter, 1990

"Our prevailing system of management has destroyed our people. People are born with intrinsic motivation, self-respect, dignity, curiosity to learn, joy in learning. The forces of destruction begin with toddlers—a prize for the best Halloween costume, grades in school, gold stars—and on up through the university."

— *W. Edwards Deming*

The bus station was nearly empty at this early hour, occupied only by a handful of travelers whose circumstances, economic or otherwise, had brought them to this particular mode of transportation. John noticed them in the way he noticed everything: with the analytical eye he had developed during years of studying operations, breaking complex systems into component parts.

There was the elderly woman clutching a battered suitcase, probably visiting grandchildren. The young man in army fatigues, heading home on leave or perhaps leaving home for the first time. The businessman whose crumpled suit suggested a fall from whatever corporate height had once afforded him better options. Each person a story, each story intersecting briefly in this fluorescent-lit terminal before diverging again into separate destinies.

John wondered what story the others saw when they looked at him. A young man in his late twenties, dressed in clothes that fell somewhere between academic and professional. Carrying an old duffel bag that spoke of family history rather than fashion choice. Looking slightly out of place, as if he belonged neither to the world of manual labor these people understood nor to the executive suites he was supposedly joining.

The truth was more complicated than any of them could guess. John Valerio was indeed Tony's grandson, heir to a legacy of factory floor wisdom that had never found its proper voice in corporate corridors. But he was also Dr. John Valerio, holder of two degrees from Boston Institute of Technology (BIT), author of a dissertation on the "failure modes of organizational change initiatives" that had won awards precisely because it asked uncomfortable questions about why well-intentioned transformations so often collapsed.

His advisor had called his work "a devastating critique of management hubris," which John had taken as high praise, coming from a woman who had spent thirty years documenting the ways organizations resisted the very changes they claimed to want.

"You've identified the pattern," she had told him at his final defense. "Now the question is whether you can break it." That question had followed him from Boston to this Syracuse bus terminal, and it would follow him through the gates of Meridian Manufacturing. Could anyone break the pattern? Could listening really change outcomes? Or were these factories, these vast machines for converting human effort into products, fundamentally resistant to the kind of transformation he hoped to achieve?

The taxi ride gave him time to think about what awaited him. David Sterling, CEO at Meridian, had been honest about the challenges, refreshingly so, compared to the corporate doublespeak John had encountered during his consulting work.

"We're dying," Sterling had said during their first phone call, with the matter-of-factness of a doctor delivering a terminal diagnosis.

"Not dramatically, not quickly, but steadily and inevitably. Every metric that matters is trending wrong. Revenue down fifteen percent over three years. Market share eroding to overseas competitors. Best workers leaving for better opportunities. The ones who stay are either too old to start over or too young to know better."

"Why bring me in?" John had asked. "Consultants haven't helped before."

"Because you're not just a consultant. You're Tony Valerio's grandson. You have degrees from the same institution that trained the efficiency experts who helped create this mess. And according to your dissertation, which I've read twice, by the way, you actually understand why transformation fails."

"Understanding why something fails doesn't mean I can make it succeed."

"No," Sterling had agreed. "But it's a better starting point than pretending the problem doesn't exist."

John watched the Syracuse skyline approach through the taxi's window, remembering his grandfather's stories about this city. Tony had loved Syracuse with the fierce loyalty of an immigrant's son, seeing in its factories and neighborhoods the promise of American opportunity even as that promise slowly faded. He had raised his family here, built his life here, given his health to the machines of Meridian

Manufacturing, and in the end, died bitter that his decades of wisdom had been ignored by men in suits who knew nothing about the work itself.

"Your grandfather was the smartest man I ever knew," John's grandmother had told him at the funeral, her voice steady despite her grief. "Not book smart, he left school at fourteen to help support his family. But wise.

"He understood things about work, about people, about what makes a factory run well or poorly. And nobody ever asked him. Nobody ever listened. He died with so much still inside him, so much that could have helped."

John had made a promise at that funeral, standing by his grandfather's grave in the frozen February ground: he would find a way to honor Tony's wisdom, to prove that the intelligence of working people mattered, to bridge the gap between those who planned work and those who performed it.

Now, approaching the gates of Meridian Manufacturing for the first time as an employee rather than a visitor, he wondered if that promise had been naive. Could one person really change the culture of an organization? Could listening really overcome decades of distrust? Could the wisdom of workers like his grandfather finally find the audience it deserved?

Whatever happened next, he was committed. There was no going back to Boston, no retreating to the safety of academic theory. This was where the ideas would be tested, where the theories would meet reality, where he would either succeed or fail in ways that mattered to real people with real lives.

He started his journey, carrying his grandfather's duffel bag and his grandfather's legacy, ready to begin.

• • •

The wind off Onondaga Lake cut through his wool peacoat, carrying the chemical tang that had haunted the shoreline for generations, Allied Chemical's legacy, they said, though the plant had been closed for years.

He could have driven. Could have flown into Hancock Airport and taken a rental.

But something about returning to Syracuse demanded this slower passage, this deliberate transition from his life in Boston to whatever waited for him at Meridian. Besides, his grandfather Tony had taken this same bus route in 1946, returning from the war to reclaim his job at the plant. The symmetry appealed to John, though he suspected Tony would have laughed at such sentimentality.

"Educated fool," Tony would have said, the way he spoke about all the college men who'd tried to fix the plant over the years. "You think your books teach you about metal and men?" Maybe they didn't. But they'd taught him enough to know Meridian was dying, hemorrhaging money and workers with equal indifference. David Sterling, the CEO who'd recruited him, had been blunt during their phone conversation: "We've got a year, maybe two, before the board forces a sale or closure. I need someone who understands operations but isn't wedded to how we've always done things. Your BIT degrees gets you in the door, but your grandfather's name, that might get the workers to listen."

John doubted that. Tony Valerio had been dead five years, and whatever goodwill his name carried had probably died with him.

The taxi driver, a Bosnian refugee named Mirko, knew Meridian. "My brother-in-law works there. Second shift. Always complaining. Says management treats them like machines." He met John's eyes in the rearview mirror. "You management?"

"Starting today."

Mirko grunted. "Good luck."

The factory sprawled along the lake's eastern shore, eight buildings in brown brick that had weathered a century of Syracuse winters. The original 1888 structure stood at the center, its windows tall and narrow like a cathedral, though whatever gods were worshipped here had long since departed. Newer additions spread in all directions, 1920s expansion, post-war boom construction, a glass and steel office complex from the 1970s that looked like it had been grafted on by aliens.

The security guard barely glanced at John's new ID badge.

"Mr. Sterling said you'd be coming. Mr. Moffitt's waiting in the old building, third floor."

The old building. Of course that's where they'd put him. Not in the executive offices with their climate control and imported furniture, but in the original structure where the radiators clanged like ghost chains and the wooden floors groaned under every step.

John climbed the narrow staircase, his footsteps echoing in the stairwell. The walls were layered with decades of paint, institution green over beige over what might have been white and decorated with faded safety posters from different eras.

"SAFETY FIRST" from the 1940s. "ZERO DEFECTS" from the 1960s. "QUALITY IS JOB ONE" from the 1980s. Each slogan a failed promise, painted over but never quite erased.

The third floor had been executive offices once, probably in Tony's day. Now its function was unclear. Storage, maybe. Archives. The kind of place where companies put things they couldn't quite throw away but didn't know what to do with.

William Moffitt's office occupied the corner, and John understood immediately that this was intentional, not punishment but privilege.

The windows faced west toward the factory floor and north toward the lake, offering a view of both where they'd been and where they were going, though which was which remained uncertain.

Will stood with his back to the door, studying something on the wall. He was smaller than John had expected, compact in the way of men who'd done physical work before moving to management. His white hair was crisp, recently cut, and his cardigan looked hand-knit. Someone cared enough to knit this man sweaters. One picture stood out: Will sitting by a river, tying a fly for fishing.

"John Valerio." Will turned, extending a hand. His grip was firm, calloused.

"Your grandfather spoke of you often. The BIT graduate and consultant. He was proud, you know. Confused as hell why anyone would study industrial engineering instead of doing actual industry, but proud."

The office was a museum. Bookshelves lined three walls, packed with volumes John recognized from his graduate studies and many he didn't. Original editions of Taylor's "Scientific Management," Follett's collected papers, Mayo's Hawthorne studies. A framed letter signed by W. Edwards Deming. Photographs covering decades: Will with men John didn't recognize, Will with men he did, Douglas McGregor at MIT, Peter Drucker at a conference, and there, in a small frame on the desk, Will with Tony Valerio, both men younger, greasier, grinning beside some piece of machinery.

"Nineteen sixty-eight," Will said, following John's gaze. "We'd just figured out how to reduce changeover time on Line 3 from four hours to ninety minutes. Your grandfather's idea, actually. Management took credit, of course. They always did back then."

"And now?"

Will's smile was sardonic. "Now they don't even pretend to listen long enough to steal ideas. They don't listen to them, and they don't listen to me. I'm seen as too chummy with the Union." He gestured to a chair, cracked leather, probably older than John, and settled behind his desk. The wood was scarred, marked with coffee rings like tree rings, each stain a year of meetings, conversations, negotiations.

"David Sterling says you're here to save us," Will said. "Young man from BIT, fresh ideas, new blood. How many saviors do you think I've seen in forty-two years here?"

John met his gaze. "How many had grandfathers who worked Line 3?"

"None," Will admitted. "But that might work against you as much as for you. These men remember Tony. They remember he died bitter, feeling betrayed by a company he'd given his life to. They might not welcome his grandson coming in as management."

Through the window, John could see the factory floor, workers moving between stations with practiced efficiency. From here, they looked like components in some vast machine, each performing their prescribed function. He thought of Anna Kowalski at Hawthorne, being watched from above, being measured and studied.

"I don't want to study them from up here," John said suddenly. "I want to be down there." Will raised an eyebrow.

"The executive offices won't like that."

"The executive offices have had forty years to fix this place. How's that worked out?" Will stood, moved to the window.

"Your grandfather said something similar once. He'd just come back from a union meeting, fighting mad. Some efficiency experts from Detroit had been hired to do time studies. Tony said, and I'll never forget this, they watch us like we're animals in a zoo. They measure our motions but never ask our thoughts."

He turned back to John. "Is that what you want to do? Ask their thoughts?"

"I want to do more than ask. I want to listen. I want to act on what I hear." Looking at the picture of Will on the wall fly fishing, John said, "I want to teach them to fish." Will was quiet for a moment, studying John with pale blue eyes that had seen decades of promises made and broken.

"There's someone you need to meet," he said finally. "Tommy Kowalski. Third generation here, like you would have been. His great-grandmother worked at Western Electric in Chicago, part of those famous Hawthorne experiments. Family legend says she told Elton Mayo himself what was really happening in that relay room."

"What was really happening?"

"They were finally being treated as human beings instead of machinery." Will pulled on a wool coat that had seen better decades.

"Come on. Tommy's on first shift. Line 3, actually. Same station your grandfather worked."

They descended through the building, three flights of stairs that transitioned from executive privilege to industrial function. The air grew thicker, warmer, filled with the scent of machine oil and hot metal. The sound built gradually, first a distant hum, then a rhythm, finally a symphony of mechanical percussion as they pushed through the double doors onto the factory floor.

The noise hit John like a physical force. Not chaos but complicated order, stamping presses, conveyor systems, pneumatic tools, each adding its voice to the industrial chorus. Workers moved through this sound like dancers who knew every beat, their bodies adapted to the rhythm through years of practice.

Line 3 stretched the length of the building's original footprint, a river of metal and motion. At station seven, a man worked alone, his movements precise, economical. He was John's age, maybe a few years older, with the kind of solid build that came from actual work rather than gym membership. His hands moved with unconscious skill, assembling components into electrical housings with a speed that seemed casual but was actually the result of perfect efficiency learned through repetition.

"Tommy," Will called out during a brief lull in the line's movement. "Got someone here to meet you."

Tommy Kowalski looked up, his expression shifting from concentration to wariness. He had his great-grandmother's eyes, John thought absurdly, though he'd only seen Anna Kowalski in a single photograph in an old management textbook, one face among six women bent over relay assemblies.

"This is John Valerio. Tony's grandson." Tommy's expression shifted again, surprise, then something harder to read. He wiped his hands on a rag that looked like it had been performing this function since the plant opened.

"Tony's grandson," Tommy repeated. Not a question, just placing the fact in some mental filing system. "Heard you were coming. BIT, right? Here to fix us?"

"Here to learn," John said.

Tommy laughed, short and sharp. "That's what they all say. Then they go back to their offices and write reports about how we're doing it all wrong. My father saw six of your type come through. Changed nothing but the shift schedules and the forms we fill out."

The line started moving again, and Tommy had to turn back to his work. But he kept talking, his voice rising over the machinery's noise.

"You know what your grandfather told my father once? This was in the seventies, during the last big efficiency push. He said, 'Eddie, they measure everything except what matters.' They count our motions but never our ideas. They calculate our output but never ask our input." His hands never stopped moving, select, position, secure, release.

Every motion necessary, nothing wasted, a kind of industrial ballet perfected over years.

"Is that still true?" John asked.

Tommy glanced at him, those inherited eyes sharp with intelligence.

"You're standing up there watching me work, asking me questions while I can't stop to answer properly. You tell me." Will touched John's arm, guiding him away from the line. As they walked, he pointed out different stations, different workers, providing a genealogy of labor, whose fathers had worked here, whose mothers had joined during the war and never left, who was third generation, who was first.

They paused near the quality inspection station, where finished assemblies were checked before shipping. The inspector, a Black woman in her fifties, worked with fierce concentration, her hands moving over each piece like a pianist testing keys.

"Rosa Washington," Will said quietly. "First Black woman hired here, 1975. Fought for that job, fought to keep it. Knows more about quality than our entire QA department, but they've never promoted her past inspector."

"Why not?"

Will gave him a look that suggested the question was either naive or a test. "You need me to explain American factory floor politics to a BIT graduate?"

They continued the tour, Will pointing out inefficiencies with casual precision, inventory stacked in walkways, machines positioned to require extra steps, quality checks that happened too late to prevent defects. Each observation came with history: when the problem started, who had tried to fix it, why it had failed.

Near the loading dock, they encountered a cluster of workers on break, smoking despite the new NO SMOKING signs, their conversation dying as management approached.

"Gentlemen," Will nodded. Several nodded back, but their eyes were on John, measuring, evaluating, categorizing.

As they headed back toward the old building, John noticed something.

"The suggestion box," he said, pointing to a wooden box mounted on the wall, its slot sealed with industrial tape, rust bleeding through its green paint.

"Sealed since 1987," Will said. "Last suggestion implemented was…" He thought for a moment. "1979, I think. Someone proposed rearranging the tool stations. Saved thirty seconds per unit. The suggester got a fifty-dollar bonus and a certificate. The company saved three hundred thousand dollars that year alone."

"Why did they stop?"

"New management. Decided workers were there to work, not make changes. That's what engineers were for. That's what consultants were for. That's what managers were for."

Will's voice carried forty years of frustration compressed into quiet words.

"They brought in experts from Japan to teach us Total Quality Management, then ignored the part about respecting worker knowledge. They hired consultants to implement Just-in-Time production, then wouldn't let workers adjust the schedules. They preached improvement while punishing anyone who admitted current processes weren't perfect."

They climbed the stairs back to Will's office. The effort left Will slightly winded, and John wondered how many more years the older man would make this climb, how many more saviors he'd be asked to orient.

"There's something you need to see," Will said once they were back in his office. He pulled out a key ring that belonged in a museum, selected a small brass key, and opened a filing cabinet that looked older than the building.

Inside were folders, hundreds of them, yellowed with age. Will pulled one out seemingly at random, opened it on the desk.

"Worker suggestions," he said. "Every one submitted since we started collecting. The company had to keep them, union contract requirement. But keeping them and reading them..." He shrugged.

John picked up a page, the handwriting careful, labored. "March 15, 1952. Anthony Valerio, Badge #3847. Subject: Repositioning of Machine Press at Station Seven."

His grandfather's suggestion. The same improvement Tommy Kowalski had been demonstrating unconsciously, how a slight repositioning would save steps, save time, save effort.

"Never implemented?" John asked, though he knew the answer.

"Never even acknowledged. That's your inheritance, John. Not just your grandfather's bitterness, but the bitterness of every worker whose ideas died in these files."

John looked through more suggestions, dates spanning decades, names representing Syracuse's ethnic history, Italian, Polish, Irish, German, African American, Puerto Rican. Each one a moment when a worker had cared enough to write down an idea, to believe it might matter. "What happened to the suggestion box program?" Will laughed, bitter and short.

"Harold Morrison happened. Our current CFO. Came in with the leveraged buyout crowd in '86. Cut everything that didn't show immediate return on investment. The suggestion program costs fifty thousand a year to administer, bonuses, processing, evaluation. He cut it. Saved fifty thousand. Cost us millions in improvements never made, but those don't show up on a balance sheet." A knock on the door interrupted them. Maria Santiago entered without waiting for permission, a compact woman with silver threading through black hair pulled back, wearing a union steward badge like armor.

"Mr. Moffitt," she nodded, then turned to John. "Mr. Valerio. I'm Maria Santiago, union representative. Heard you were touring the floor."

"Word travels fast," John said.
"It's a factory, everything echoes." She studied him with dark eyes that had seen too many management initiatives.

"My father worked with your grandfather. They were friends, or as much as a Mexican could be friends with an Italian in those days. He said Tony Valerio was the only supervisor who ever really listened."

"He wasn't a supervisor," John corrected.

"He was a supervisor," Maria interrupted. "Nineteen seventy-one through seventy-three. They promoted him, then demoted him when he wouldn't enforce the new productivity standards. Said he was too sympathetic to worker concerns. My father kept the letter they made Tony sign, acknowledging his demotion. Want to see it?"

John felt something cold settle in his stomach. His grandfather had never mentioned being a supervisor, never mentioned being demoted.

Another inherited bitterness.

"Yes," he said. "I want to see it." Maria smiled, sharp and knowing.

"Good. Come to the union hall tomorrow, at 5 AM. We'll talk before first shift. You can hear what the workers really think when management isn't listening." She left without waiting for a response. Will chuckled.

"Maria doesn't trust easily. Her father led the seventy-eight strike. Company promised worker participation in exchange for wage concessions. Workers gave the concessions. Company forgot the participation. Classic bait and switch."

Through the window, the afternoon shift was arriving, streams of workers converging on the plant. John watched them punch in at the time clock, the same ritual his grandfather had performed thousands of times.

"I want to move my desk down there across from the Union office," John said suddenly. "To the floor."

Will's eyebrows rose. "Morrison will have a fit."

"Then Morrison can fire me. But if I'm going to understand what's wrong here, I can't do it from three floors up."

Will was quiet for a moment, then moved to his bookshelf. He pulled out a worn volume, handed it to John.

"Mary Parker Follett. *Dynamic Administration*. First edition, 1942. Read the chapter on power-with versus power-over. Then tell me if you still want to move to the floor."

The book felt substantial in John's hands, its cloth cover worn smooth by decades of handling. Inside the front cover, someone had written in fountain pen "To Will, Remember, integration not domination. Doug McGregor, 1961."

"You knew McGregor?"

"I was his student. Last class he taught at MIT before he died. He used to say that every organization faces a choice: treat workers as problems to be controlled or partners to be developed. Most choose control because it feels safer." Will moved back to the window.

"Your grandfather understood partnership instinctively. That's why they had to break him."

"They didn't break him," John protested. "He worked here until..."

"They broke him," Will repeated quietly. "When they demoted him, when they ignored his suggestions, when they made him watch younger men with degrees make mistakes he could have prevented. They broke his spirit if not his body. The question is whether you can avoid the same fate."

The factory whistle blew at 4:30, shift change in thirty minutes. The sound echoed across the lake, as it had for a century, calling workers to their stations, marking time in increments of labor.

"There's one more thing," Will said, moving to a closet John hadn't noticed. Inside, covered in dust, was a wooden crate. Will pulled it out with effort, set it on his desk, and pried open the top.

Inside were hundreds of suggestions, not filed neatly but thrown together, some typed, most handwritten, dates ranging from the 1980s to just last year.

"The suggestion box wasn't empty when they sealed it," Will explained. "Workers kept sliding suggestions under the tape, through the gaps. No one ever opened it officially, but the janitor, old Pete Wojcik, collected them, brought them to me. Couldn't bring myself to throw them away."

John picked up a recent one, dated just three months ago. The handwriting was neat, careful: "If we moved the inspection station closer to assembly, we could catch defects before they compound. Signed, T. Kowalski." Tommy's suggestion. The same principle his great-grandmother had understood at Hawthorne, bring inspection to the source, make quality everyone's responsibility.

"How many of these would have worked?" John asked.

"Most of them. Workers aren't stupid, John. They see problems we can't see from up here. They know solutions we'd never think of in meeting rooms. But acknowledging that means admitting our whole management structure is built on a lie, the lie that thinking is separate from doing, that intelligence flows down from above."

The room was growing dark, February evening falling fast. Will turned on a desk lamp, its yellow light making the office feel even more like a museum after closing.

"You want some advice?" Will asked.

"Always."

"Don't try to change everything at once. I tried that a few times. Don't come in with grand theories and BIT solutions. Start small. One station, one worker, one suggestion. Show them you can listen, really listen, and act on what you hear. Your grandfather's name might get you in the door, but you'll have to earn their trust one small change at a time." Will smiled.

"Old factory expression. Sometimes the biggest changes come from the smallest adjustments. Moving a machine six inches to save a step. Adjusting a process by six seconds to prevent a defect. Workers know these six-inch improvements, but management always wants six-foot leaps."

John stood to leave, holding Follett's book.

"Thank you. For the history lesson."

"History isn't past here," Will said. "Every worker carries their father's stories, their grandfather's defeats. Every suggestion ignored becomes a family legend of disrespect. You're not just managing a factory, John. You're managing a century of accumulated wisdom and wounded pride. You get the Union relationship that you deserve."

As John left the building, the night shift was arriving. He recognized some faces from the morning, double-shifters, working sixteen hours to make ends meet. They looked exhausted already, and their shift hadn't even started.

At the gate, he turned back to look at the plant, lit now by sodium lights that turned everything orange. Somewhere in there, Tommy Kowalski was finishing his shift. Rosa Washington was inspecting the day's last batch. And Pete Wojcik was collecting suggestions that would never be read.

His grandfather had worked here for thirty-seven years, been promoted and demoted, offered ideas that were ignored, and died believing his wisdom didn't matter. John carried that inheritance along with his BIT degree, the weight of accumulated disappointment, the possibility of redemption.

The bus back to his hotel passed through the old neighborhoods, Little Italy, Polish Town, the North Side where Black families had settled during the Great Migration. Each neighborhood had sent its workers to Meridian, each family had its stories of pride and frustration, hope and disappointment.

In his hotel room, John opened Follett's book to the chapter Will had mentioned. Her words, written in the 1920s, felt immediate:

"The essential feature of a common purpose is not that it should be a common purpose, but that it should be a purpose common to each..."

"Integration involves invention, and the clever thing is to recognize this, and not to let one's thinking stay within the boundaries of two alternatives which are mutually exclusive."

He thought of Tommy Kowalski, hands moving with perfect efficiency, suggesting improvements that would never be heard. He thought of his grandfather, demoted for listening too well. He thought of Will Moffitt, keeping years of ignored suggestions in a closet, unable to throw away all that accumulated wisdom.

Tomorrow he would meet Maria Santiago at the union hall. Tomorrow he would start moving his office to the factory floor. Tomorrow he would begin the work of listening, of inclusion.

But tonight, he sat with Follett's book and the weight of inheritance, not just his grandfather's, but Anna Kowalski's at Hawthorne, Tommy's at his station, Rosa Washington's at her inspection bench. All of them waiting, after decades of silence, for someone to finally ask their thoughts and write them down like they mattered. To include them in problem solving.

Because they did matter. They had always mattered.

John understood the revolution wouldn't begin with grand gestures or BIT theories. It would begin with small adjustments that proved change was possible, one voice heard that encouraged others to speak.

Outside, snow began to fall on Syracuse, covering the city in temporary white, making everything seem possible, even redemption.

Even transformation.

Six inch moves at a time.

LESSONS LEARNED

Why 70% of Transformations Fail

Research consistently shows that the majority of organizational change initiatives fail to achieve their intended goals. Valerio's dissertation research identified the pattern: most change efforts fail because they don't genuinely engage the people who have to make them work. Organizations impose change from above rather than eliciting it from within, treating workers as obstacles to be overcome rather than partners to be enlisted.

Douglas McGregor's Theory X and Theory Y

McGregor (1960) described two fundamentally different assumptions about human motivation. Theory X assumes workers are lazy, need control, and avoid responsibility. Theory Y assumes workers are self-motivated, seek responsibility, and want to contribute. The treatment Tony Valerio received, demoted for being 'too sympathetic to worker concerns,' reflects Theory X assumptions so deeply embedded in organizational culture that they persisted even when evidence contradicted them.

Creating Value Connection

As Rizzo explains in *Creating Value*, the choice between treating workers as problems or partners is not merely philosophical but has concrete consequences for organizational performance. Companies that choose partnership consistently outperform those that choose control, not despite their worker focus but because of it.

"Top-down initiatives fade when consultants leave or leaders change. Sustainable improvement requires embedding problem-solving capability in the workforce itself."

CHAPTER 2

The Ghost of Frederick Taylor

"It seems to me that whereas power usually means power-over, the power of some person or group over some other person or group, it is possible to develop the conception of power-with, a jointly developed power, a co-active, not a coercive power." — Mary Parker Follett

The union hall occupied a converted warehouse three blocks from the plant, its industrial origins evident in the high ceilings and exposed pipes that no amount of paneling could disguise. John had come here at Will's suggestion, understanding that any successful transformation would require the union's cooperation, or at least its grudging acceptance.

Maria Santiago met him at the door, her skepticism evident before she spoke a single word. At forty-seven, she had been union president for three terms, having worked her way up from the assembly line through positions of increasing responsibility. Her reputation preceded her: tough, smart, uncompromising, and absolutely devoted to the workers she represented.

"So you're the miracle worker," she said, the phrase delivered with a tone that made clear her opinion of miracles. "Sterling's latest attempt to fix things without actually changing anything."

"I'm here to listen," John said.

"Everyone's here to listen. Then they go back to their offices and do whatever they were going to do anyway." She led him through the hall's main room, past tables where workers gathered for meetings, past bulletin boards covered with announcements and grievances, past a wall of photographs documenting the union's history, strikes and negotiations, victories and defeats, faces that had aged or disappeared over the decades.

They settled in her office, a small room made smaller by filing cabinets stuffed with records of every contract, every dispute, every broken promise made and unmade over forty years of labor-management relations.

Maria pulled out a folder and set it on the desk between them.

"This is Miguel Santos. Thirty-two years at Meridian, second-generation worker, his mother was one of the first women hired in the plant, back in '65. He filed a suggestion about repositioning the safety guards on the stamping press to reduce changeover time. Want to guess what happened?" John shook his head.

"Nothing. Not even an acknowledgment that the suggestion was received. He followed up three times, got the same response each time: 'Under review.' Then the suggestion system was 'reorganized', which meant all the old suggestions disappeared into some filing cabinet and were never seen again."

She opened the folder, revealing a handwritten form covered in precise, engineering-quality drawings. Miguel's idea was elegant in its simplicity, a repositioning of safety interlocks that would allow operators to access tools without disabling the entire safety system during changeovers.

"This would have saved at least twenty minutes per changeover," Maria said. "Multiplied by three changeovers per shift, three shifts per day, five days per week, fifty weeks per year. That's..." She paused, calculating.

"Seventy-five hundred hours per year. If we assume a conservative value of twenty dollars per hour in productivity terms, that's a hundred and fifty thousand dollars annually. That's what ignoring Miguel's idea has cost this company. And Miguel's just one worker with one idea."

"Multiply that across hundreds of workers, thousands of ideas, decade after decade..." She let the implication hang in the air.

John studied the diagram, recognizing the quality of thought behind it. This wasn't a casual suggestion; this was careful analysis by someone who understood both the machinery and the workflow, someone who had spent years observing inefficiencies that management either couldn't see or chose not to address.

"May I speak with Miguel?" Maria's expression shifted slightly, not quite softening, but losing some of its edge.

"He's on second shift. Comes in at two. But I should warn you: he's not optimistic about management's capacity for change. None of us are."

"I understand. But I'd like to try anyway." Maria studied him for a long moment, her eyes searching for something, sincerity, perhaps, or the telltale signs of corporate manipulation she had learned to recognize over decades of negotiation.

Whatever she found seemed to satisfy her, at least provisionally.

"I'll set it up. But John, can I call you John? If you're playing games with these people, if you're just gathering ammunition for the next round of layoffs or using their ideas without giving credit, I will make your life very difficult. These workers have been burned too many times to forgive another betrayal."

"I understand," John said again. "And I'm not here to betray anyone. I'm here because I believe their wisdom matters. I'm here because my grandfather died believing no one would ever listen. I'm here because someone has to prove that things can be different."

Maria nodded slowly. "We'll see. Words are easy. Action is harder. Show me actions, and maybe, maybe, we can work together." It was, John realized, the best he could hope for. Trust would have to be earned, one action at a time, one kept promise at a time. The path forward would be slow, difficult, and fraught with the accumulated distrust of generations.

But it was a path. And that was more than he had expected.

• • •

February in Syracuse was a month designed to break spirits. The lake-effect snow that had started the night before continued through dawn, muffling the city in white silence. John arrived at the union hall at 4:45 AM, fifteen minutes early for his second visit, but Maria Santiago was already there, the lights on, coffee brewing in an industrial percolator that looked like it had served every union meeting since the hall was built.

"Punctual," she said without looking up from the papers she was arranging. "Your grandfather was always early too. Said it was the one thing management couldn't hold against him."

The union hall occupied a narrow building on North Salina Street, squeezed between a Polish bakery and a check-cashing store. The main room held rows of folding chairs facing a small stage, the walls decorated with photographs of strikes, victories, defeats, the visual history of Syracuse labor.

John recognized one photo immediately: the 1978 strike, workers holding signs in the snow, his grandfather among them, looking uncomfortable on the management side of the line.

"That must have been hard for him," Maria said, following his gaze. "Tony believed in the company, even after they demoted him. Believed it could be better. The strike broke something in him." She poured coffee into two chipped mugs, handed one to John. It was strong enough to strip paint, hot enough to burn away the morning cold.

"Sit," she commanded, pointing to a wooden table scarred by decades of use. From her bag, she pulled a leather journal, its pages yellowed and brittle.

"My father's diary. Want to know what really happened here? Read this."

The entry was dated March 15, 1978: "Tony Valerio came to the line today, trying to explain management's position. The men wouldn't look at him. This is the same Tony who fought for us when he was supervisor, who got fired for refusing to enforce impossible quotas. Now he has to defend the very policies he opposed. I see it killing him, poco a poco. The company owns his body eight hours a day, but now they want his soul too."

John's throat tightened. His grandfather had never spoken of this period, had deflected questions about the strike with vague comments about "difficult times."

"There's more," Maria said, flipping pages. "September 1956. My father was young then, just started at the plant. The efficiency experts are back. Men in white shirts with stopwatches, following us like shadows. They time everything, how long to pick up a tool, how long to tighten a bolt, how long to breathe. Stefan Kowalski's son Eddie jokes they'll time our bathroom breaks next.

"But it's not funny when they announce the new standards: 20% more output with 15% fewer workers. The experts say we've been wasting time. They've never done the work, but they know we're doing it wrong."

"Nineteen fifty-six," John said. "The same year Will Moffitt tried to implement human relations programs."

Maria's smile was bitter. "Two programs running parallel, one treating workers like machines to be optimized, one pretending to care about their feelings. The contradiction never occurred to management. Or maybe it did, and they just didn't care."

The door opened, bringing a gust of cold air and Tommy Kowalski, stamping snow from his boots. He stopped when he saw John.

"Management at the union hall. That's either very brave or very stupid."

"Maybe both," John admitted.

Tommy poured himself coffee and joined them at the table. Up close, without the noise and motion of the factory floor, John could see the intelligence in his eyes more clearly, the careful way he assessed everything before speaking.

"Maria says you want to hear what workers really think," Tommy said.

"Here's what I think: you're the seventh management savior I've seen. The first one came when I was twelve, my dad brought me to the plant during school break. Some hotshot from Harvard, full of theories about Quality Circles. Lasted six months. The second came in '83, preaching Japanese management. Lasted eight months. Should I go on?"

"What made them fail?" Tommy and Maria exchanged glances.

"You really don't know?" Tommy asked. "BIT didn't teach you about organizational resistance?"

"BIT taught me theory. I'm asking about practice." Tommy leaned back, studying John.

"Alright. I'll tell you why they failed. They came in with solutions to problems they didn't understand. They imposed changes without asking the people doing the work. And when things got hard, when Management pushed back, when the board complained about quarterly numbers, when workers didn't immediately embrace their brilliant ideas, they gave up and moved on to the next company, the next challenge."

"Your grandfather was different," Maria added. "When he was supervisor, he came to the floor every day. Not to watch us like the time-study men, but to work alongside us when someone called in sick, to understand what we faced. That's why his demotion hurt so much. The company punished him for actually knowing the work."

The door opened again, and more workers entered, early arrivals for the day shift. They nodded at Maria and Tommy, eyed John with suspicion.

Word had already spread: Tony Valerio's grandson, the Boston Institute of Technology engineer, and another savior come to fix them.

"Show him the room," Maria told Tommy.

Tommy hesitated, then stood. "Come on." They went upstairs, the old wooden steps creaking under their weight.

The second floor was storage, boxes of grievances, negotiation records, the documented history of labor-management conflict. Tommy led him to a door at the far end, pulled out a key.

"We call this the Museum of Failed Promises," he said.

The room was filled with artifacts from improvement initiatives: binders from Quality Circle training, posters from Total Quality Management campaigns, manuals from Statistical Process Control implementations.

Each one gathering dust, each one representing hope that had curdled into cynicism.

"Nineteen eighty-two," Tommy said, picking up a Certificate of Recognition. "I suggested a way to reduce setup time on the punch press. They gave me this certificate and fifty dollars. The improvement saved them three hundred thousand a year. When I asked for a raise, they said certificates don't go in personnel files."

He picked up another item, a hard hat with "SAFETY TEAM LEADER" stenciled on it.

"Nineteen eighty-seven. They made me safety team leader after I identified seventeen hazards in my area. I fixed them all. Injury rates dropped sixty percent. When layoffs came six months later, being safety team leader didn't protect my job. I survived, but the message was clear: contributions don't count when numbers are bad."

John noticed a photograph on the wall, workers arranged in rows, holding a banner: MERIDIAN IMPROVEMENT TEAM 1968.

"That's my dad," Tommy pointed to a young man in the front row. "Eddie Kowalski. He believed in continuous improvement before it had a fancy name. See the man next to him? That's your grandfather. They worked together to redesign the workflow on Line 3. Saved the company millions over the years."

"What happened to the program?"

"Same thing that happens to all programs. New management came in and decided workers thinking was dangerous. Might lead to bad decisions. Better to have them just follow orders."

They descended back to the main hall, which was filling now with workers grabbing coffee before their shift. The conversation died as John entered, then resumed in lower tones. He caught fragments:

"Another college boy..."

"Tony's grandson..."

"How long before he gives up?"

An older woman approached: Rosa Washington, the quality inspector from Line 3.

"Mr. Valerio," she said formally. "I knew your grandfather. He was the only supervisor who ever asked my opinion about quality problems. When they demoted him, I started keeping my own records, my own data. Management doesn't want to hear what I know, but I keep tracking anyway."

"Why?" John asked.

Her smile was sad and proud simultaneously. "Because someday, someone might actually listen. And when they do, I'll have twenty years of evidence about what's really wrong and how to fix it."

"I'd like to see those records."

She studied him for a long moment. "I'll think about it."

The workers began filing out, heading for the plant. John walked with them, feeling like an imposter in his wool coat among their Carhartt jackets. The snow had stopped, but the wind off the lake was brutal, cutting through layers of clothing.

At the plant, Harold Morrison stood at the executive entrance, his black Town Car idling behind him. The CFO was thin to the point of gauntness, his expensive suit hanging on his frame like ambition itself.

"Mr. Valerio," Morrison's voice carried despite the wind. "We need to talk."

John followed him inside, up to the executive floor he'd avoided yesterday. Morrison's office was everything Will Moffitt's wasn't, modern, sterile, dominated by spreadsheets and financial projections pinned to every wall.

"I understand you're planning to move your office, a standup desk, to the factory floor," Morrison said without preamble. "I can't allow that."

"I don't recall asking permission."

Morrison's smile was thin. "You don't understand how things work here. I've been CFO for fifteen years. I've outlasted four presidents, three COOs, and countless improvement initiatives. You know why? Because I keep this company profitable enough to survive."

"Profitable? We're losing money."

"We're managing decline. There's a difference." Morrison moved to his whiteboard, covered in numbers. "Labor costs: thirty-two percent of revenue. Industry standard: twenty-two percent. We need to cut workforce by forty percent to be competitive."

"Or we could improve productivity by forty percent."

Morrison laughed, a sound like paper crumpling. "With what? Worker suggestions? I've seen that fantasy before. In 1987, when I eliminated the suggestion program, we were spending fifty thousand a year on administration. The so-called savings were mostly imaginary, workers claiming credit for improvements that would have happened anyway or never happened."

"Will Moffitt says…"

"Will Moffitt is a romantic. He still believes in McGregor's Theory Y, and still thinks workers want to contribute. I've been here fifteen years, Mr. Valerio. Workers want paychecks and job security. Period. They'll tell you what you want to hear if they think it protects their jobs."

John thought of Rosa Washington, keeping quality records for twenty years without recognition. Tommy Kowalski, sliding suggestions under the sealed box. His grandfather, demoted for listening too well.

"You're wrong," John said quietly.

Morrison's face flushed. "I'm trying to save this company. When the board forces a sale, we could preserve maybe sixty percent of the jobs if we've shown improvement in labor costs. Or we can indulge your fantasies about worker empowerment and watch the whole place get shuttered. Your choice."

John left without responding, taking the stairs down to the factory floor. The morning shift was in full swing, the machinery's rhythm like a heartbeat. He found Will Moffitt at Line 3, talking with Tommy.

"Morrison?" Will asked, reading John's expression.

"He wants forty percent workforce reduction." Tommy laughed bitterly.

"Of course he does. It's the only idea he's ever had. There's something you need to see," Will said. He led them to a storage area behind Line 3, pulled back a tarp. Underneath was an old machine, pristine despite its age.

"Cincinnati Milling Machine, 1952," Will said. "Your grandfather operated this for fifteen years. See these modifications?"

He pointed to various adjustments, improvements, and additions. "Tony did these. Increased output thirty percent, improved quality, reduced operator fatigue. He documented everything, submitted formal improvement reports."

"What happened?"

"Engineering department claimed credit. Tony got a ten-dollar bonus. The modifications were rolled out plant-wide, probably saved millions over the years. Tony's name appears nowhere in the records."

John ran his hand over the machine, feeling the smooth metal worn by his grandfather's hands. How many improvements had died here? How many ideas had been stolen, ignored, suppressed?

"I want to move this machine," John said suddenly. "Put it where people can see it. A reminder of what workers can do when they're allowed to think, to act."

Tommy snorted. "Morrison will never approve that."

"I'm not asking Morrison." That afternoon, John made good on his promise. With Will's help and the bemused cooperation of maintenance, they cleared a space near the main floor entrance and moved Tony Valerio's modified machine into position.

John made and attached a placard: This machine was improved by Anthony Valerio, Badge #3847, 1952-1967. His modifications increased productivity by 30% and became plant standard.

"This is what happens when we empower workers."

By shift change, workers were stopping to look, to read, to remember. Older workers shared stories of Tony, of their own improvements, of ideas that had been ignored.

Morrison appeared within an hour, enraged. "You have no authority."

"I have the authority to recognize worker contributions," John interrupted. "Unless you want to explicitly forbid that?"

Morrison looked around at the gathered workers, seething, calculating the optics.

"This changes nothing," he said finally. "Six months, Mr. Valerio. Show me numbers or start planning layoffs." As Morrison retreated to his executive floor, Rosa Washington approached John.

In her hands was a thick binder, worn from handling.

"Twenty years of quality data," she said simply. "Every defect, every pattern, every solution that could have prevented problems. No one ever asked for it before."

John took the binder, feeling its weight, not just of paper but of years of unrecognized expertise.

"Tomorrow," he said, "we start team workshops. You, Tommy, whoever wants to participate. We're going to document every improvement idea, test them, and implement them. And this time, the workers who suggest them will get credit."

"Morrison won't allow it," Tommy said.

"Morrison doesn't have to allow it. David Sterling hired me to save this plant. That's what I'm going to do."

That evening, John set up his new office, a standup desk on the factory floor, positioned where he could see Line 3 and across from a Union office. He pinned his grandfather's 1952 suggestion on the wall, next to a photo Will had given him of Tony at his machine.

As second shift began, workers passed by, curious but wary. Some nodded, a few stopped to talk. An older Polish worker named Stan Pomorski shared a story about Tony teaching him to read blueprints. A younger woman, Jennifer Chen, fresh from engineering school, admitted she'd chosen Meridian because her father had worked here with Tony.

"He always said Tony Valerio was the only supervisor who respected worker intelligence," she said. "I wanted to work somewhere that had that history, even if it was buried."

As the shift wore on, John began to understand the rhythm of the floor, not just the mechanical rhythm but the human one. The way workers communicated without words, the subtle adjustments they made to keep machines running, the accumulated knowledge that no time-study could capture.

Around midnight, he found a box on his desk. Inside were suggestions, dozens of them, some dating back years.

A note was attached: "We never stopped thinking. We just stopped believing anyone cared."

John spread the suggestions across his desk, reading by the harsh fluorescent light. Improvements to workflow, safety enhancements, quality fixes, practical solutions to real problems from the people who faced them every day.

One caught his eye, written in careful script: "If we moved the inspection station closer to assembly, we could catch defects immediately instead of after they compound." T. Kowalski, 1993.

Will had mentioned the importance of small improvements. Small changes that could cascade into transformation.

John looked up to find Tommy watching him from Line 3. "That small a move?" John called out over the machinery noise.

Tommy nodded, a smile ghosting across his face. "Sometimes that's all it takes. The question is whether anyone's brave enough to move it."

John stood, grabbed a measuring tape from the tool station. "Show me exactly where it should go."

For the next hour, Tommy explained his idea, not just the move but the reasoning behind it, the workflow analysis he'd done in his head over years of observation. Other workers drifted over during breaks, adding their perspectives, building on Tommy's concept.

By 2 AM, they had a plan. Not just for moving the inspection station but for reorganizing the entire flow of Line 3. It would cost almost nothing to implement but could reduce defects by forty percent, according to Rosa Washington's data.

"We'll need Morrison's approval," someone said.

"No," John replied. "We need results. We implement it this weekend, during maintenance downtime. If it works, Morrison can argue with success."

The workers exchanged glances, surprise, hope, skepticism all mixed together.

"You're risking your job," Tommy said.

John thought of his grandfather, demoted for listening too well, dying bitter but unbroken. He thought of Anna Kowalski at Hawthorne, finally being asked her opinion. He thought of all the suggestions, smoldering in boxes and filing cabinets, all the wisdom ignored.

"Some things are worth the risk," he said.

As the night shift ended and dawn approached, John remained at his floor desk, planning the workshop that would begin in a few hours. Through the windows, he could see snow beginning to fall again, covering Syracuse in another layer of white.

But inside the plant, something was stirring. Workers who hadn't made suggestions in years were writing down ideas. Rosa Washington was organizing her quality data for presentation. Tommy was sketching workflow diagrams.

The ghost of Frederick Taylor still haunted the factory, the legacy of treating workers as automatons, of measuring motion but ignoring minds.

But other ghosts were stirring too: Tony Valerio at his modified machine, Eddie Kowalski with his continuous improvement ideas. All the workers whose intelligence had been suppressed but never extinguished.

Change would come, John realized, not through grand theories or management initiatives, but through accumulation, one small change at a time, one suggestion implemented, one worker heard. The transformation wouldn't be announced in boardrooms or documented in strategic plans. It would happen in the workplace, in the space between what was and what could be.

Morrison was right about one thing: they had six months. But John was beginning to understand that six months was plenty of time for small changes to add up to transformation.

The question was no longer whether workers had ideas worth hearing.

The question was whether management had the courage to listen.

LESSONS LEARNED

Frederick Taylor's Lasting Shadow

Frederick Winslow Taylor's scientific management (1911) revolutionized American industry by separating thinking from doing. Engineers would design the 'one best way' to perform each task, and workers would execute those designs without deviation. While this approach achieved efficiency gains, it also created a fundamental disconnect: the assumption that workers were 'just hands' rather than thinking human beings.

The Suggestion Box as Symbol

The sealed suggestion box, locked since 1987 with worker ideas still sliding through the gaps in the tape, represents the paradox of organizations that create mechanisms for participation while simultaneously signaling that participation doesn't matter. The forms are collected but no one reads them. The procedures exist but nothing changes.

Creating Value Connection

In *Creating Value*, Rizzo describes the fundamental choice every organization faces: extract value from workers or create value with them. Value extraction, the Taylor-inspired approach, treats workers as interchangeable inputs to be optimized. Value creation treats workers as unique sources of knowledge and capability.

"Value creation invests in people, builds problem-solving capacity, and generates sustainable success for all stakeholders."

CHAPTER 3

Echoes of Hawthorne

"One friend, one person who is truly understanding, who takes the trouble to listen to us as we consider our problem, can change our whole outlook on the world." — Elton Mayo

The first formal team workshop, also called kaizen in today's management books, took place on a Tuesday morning, in a conference room that had been chosen specifically for its neutrality. John had spent the previous week planning every detail, sensing that the first impression would determine whether workers engaged or withdrew.

Tommy Kowalski arrived early, which John took as a hopeful sign. The cynical worker from their first meeting had agreed to participate, though with the explicit warning that "I'm here to see if you're different from the others, not because I think you will be."

The other participants filtered in over the next fifteen minutes: Rosa Washington, her quality inspector's eye already cataloging the room's details; Stefan, Tommy's cousin, John had learned, who worked the night shift and had taken vacation time to attend; Maria Santiago, representing the union's interest in whatever was about to happen; and three workers from different lines whose reputations for thoughtfulness had led to their selection.

Will Moffitt sat in the corner, observing but not participating, a conscious choice, John knew, to remove the weight of management authority from the conversation. His presence was intended as support, not surveillance.

John launched directly into the heart of the matter: "I'm not here to tell you what's wrong with Meridian. You know that better than I ever could. I'm here to ask what you think could make it better, and to commit, publicly, with witnesses, that your ideas will be taken seriously."

The skepticism in the room was palpable, a physical presence that seemed to thicken the air. These workers had heard promises before. They had submitted suggestions that disappeared into bureaucratic black holes. They had watched consultants come and go, each one promising transformation and delivering nothing but new forms to fill out.

"What makes this different?" Rosa asked, her voice carrying the weight of twenty years of experience. "I've seen six 'improvement initiatives' in my time here. Each one started with a meeting just like this. Each one ended with nothing changed except a long list that never got implemented."

John nodded, acknowledging the validity of her question. "What makes this different is that I'm not going to tell you what to do. I'm going to ask what you think should be done, and then I'm going to help make it happen. Not study it. Not analyze it. Not write a report recommending further study. Actually, give it a try, with your involvement every step of the way."

"And if management doesn't like what we suggest?" Stefan asked. The night shift worker had the tired eyes of someone who had learned to distrust daylight promises.

"Then we document why they rejected it, and we keep pushing. I'm not naive enough to think every idea will be implemented. But I am committed to ensuring that every idea gets a fair hearing, and every rejection comes with a real explanation."

The conversation that followed lasted three hours, far longer than John had planned, but he made no move to cut it short. The workers talked about inefficiencies they had observed for years: tools stored in illogical locations, quality checks that happened too late in the process to prevent defects, communication breakdowns between shifts that led to repeated mistakes. Root causes discovered without formality.

Tommy described a problem with the inspection station that had bothered him for months. "The light is in the wrong place," he said, gesturing as he spoke. "We have to hold each piece up at an angle to see the finish properly. Costs maybe ten seconds per piece, but multiply that across a thousand pieces a day..."

"Why hasn't anyone fixed it?" John asked.

"Because we'd have to file a facilities request, which goes to maintenance, which has a six-week backlog, and by the time they get around to looking at it, someone's decided the budget doesn't allow for 'non-essential modifications.'"

Tommy's voice carried years of frustration. "It's not that nobody cares. It's that the system makes caring almost impossible."

John made a note, then looked up at the group. "What if we just fixed it ourselves? Moved the light, tested whether it makes a difference, documented the results?"

The silence that followed was charged with something John hadn't expected: hope, fragile and cautious, but unmistakably present.

"You mean actually do something?" Rosa asked. "Without three months of approvals and studies and cost-benefit analyses?"

"I mean actually do something. Today if possible. Tomorrow at the latest."

Tommy and Stefan exchanged a glance that communicated years of shared experience. Then Tommy nodded slowly. "The inspection station's in my area. If you're serious, I can show you what needs to change."

"I am serious," John said. "Let's go look at it right now." The workshop ended not with a formal conclusion but with a procession to the factory floor, where seven workers and one manager stood around an inspection station and talked about light angles and sight lines and the accumulated wisdom of years spent doing work that others only studied from a distance.

It was, John realized, exactly what Mary Parker Follett had witnessed at Hawthorne seventy years earlier. Not a revolution, but a recognition.

Not a transformation, but a beginning.

The light was moved that afternoon. The improvement in inspection time was documented that evening. And somewhere in the filing cabinets of Meridian Manufacturing, a new kind of record began to accumulate. Not suggestions ignored, but changes implemented, wisdom honored, workers heard.

The revolution, such as it was, had begun with a light bulb.

• • •

Spring came reluctantly to Syracuse that year, as if winter itself had grown comfortable in the gray streets and frozen lake. By early April, the snow had finally retreated to dirty piles in parking lot corners, and the first green shoots appeared in the small patch of earth outside the factory that someone had optimistically designated a "memorial garden" for past workers.

John had been at Meridian for two months now, and his desk on the factory floor had evolved from curiosity to fixture. Workers had started leaving things on it, suggestions, yes, but also coffee, homemade pierogis from someone's grandmother, a worn Polish-English dictionary that Stan Pomorski thought might help John understand the older workers better.

The improvement of the inspection station had worked. Defects on Line 3 dropped forty-one percent in three weeks. Morrison had claimed credit for the "management-initiated optimization," but the workers knew the truth. More importantly, they'd seen John and Tommy move the station themselves on a Saturday, seen John covered in grease and sweat, doing actual work.

Now, on a Thursday morning that smelled of machine oil and possibility, Will Moffitt appeared at John's desk carrying two items: a first edition of Mary Parker Follett's *Dynamic Administration* and a manila folder so old it had gone soft as cloth.

"Gift and a loan," Will said, setting them down carefully. The book's binding was broken, held together with tape that had yellowed to amber.

"The book is yours. Douglas McGregor gave it to me in 1961, and I'm giving it to you. The folder is on loan from someone who wants to remain anonymous for now."

John opened the folder. Inside were photographs from the Hawthorne Works, the Western Electric plant in Chicago. Not the official photos he'd seen in textbooks, but personal snapshots. Workers at their stations, at lunch, at company picnics. In several, he recognized a young woman who had to be Anna Kowalski.

"Where did these come from?"

"Anna's daughter, Catherine. She lives in Solvay now, in the Polish nursing home. Tommy's grandmother. She's ninety-three, sharp as ever, and she wants to meet you."

"Why?"

"Because she thinks what's happening here, what you're trying to do, is what her mother always hoped would happen. Anna died believing the Hawthorne experiments would change everything. Catherine wants to know if her mother was just seventy years too early."

John studied the photographs. Anna Kowalski looked directly at the camera in each one, her gaze steady and intelligent. In one photo, she stood next to a tall man in a three-piece suit who had to be Elton Mayo.

Anna wasn't smiling, but there was something in her expression, vindication, maybe, or hope.

"I'll go see her," John said. "But first, we have another workshop."

The workshop. Their formal attempt to apply what John had learned from his studies, from the workers, from his grandfather's ghost. They'd converted a section of the old cafeteria into what Jennifer Chen had dubbed the War Room, walls covered with brown paper, boxes of colored markers, decades of production data that Rosa Washington had been compiling.

The team assembled at seven: Tommy Kowalski, Rosa Washington, Jennifer Chen, Bobby Santos from maintenance, Stan Pomorski from second shift, and surprisingly, Stefan Pomorski, Stan's nephew and Harold Morrison's plant controller.

"I'm not here as Morrison's spy," Stefan said immediately, preempting the obvious concern. "I'm here because I've been cooking the books for five years to make this place look worse than it is, and I'm tired of lying."

The room went silent. Tommy was the first to speak. "Cooking them how?" Stefan pulled out a laptop, probably the only one on the factory floor.

"Morrison has me allocate overhead in ways that make production look expensive. Every improvement you make, I find a way to hide it in the numbers. The forty-one percent defect reduction on Line 3? In Morrison's reports to the board, it shows as increased inspection costs."

"Why are you telling us this?" Rosa asked.

"Because my grandfather worked here. My uncle works here. My kids will probably work here unless Morrison succeeds in destroying it for a leveraged buyout."

John felt the room shift, like a machine clicking into gear. This wasn't just about process improvement anymore. This was about survival.

"Show us," he said.

For the next hour, Stefan walked them through the true financial picture. The plant wasn't hemorrhaging money. It was barely breaking even, held down by deliberate inefficiencies and Morrison's refusal to invest in improvements.

"If we implemented just the suggestions submitted in the last year," Stefan said, "we could improve margins by twelve percent. That's without any capital investment, just process improvements."

"Then why doesn't Morrison…" Jennifer began, then stopped.

"He wants the plant to fail?"

"I think he wants to buy it," Will Moffitt said from the doorway. None of them had heard him arrive.

Tommy slammed his fist on the table. "That son of a bitch has been sabotaging us for a few years?"

"Longer," Will said. "But proving it and stopping it are different things."

John stood, moved to the brown paper covering the walls. "Then we prove this place can work. We show the board what's possible when workers and the Union are actually allowed to improve things."

He picked up a marker. "Rosa, tell us about quality problems."

For the next six hours, they mapped everything. Rosa's quality data revealed patterns no one had seen: defects clustered at specific times, specific stations, specific conditions. Bobby identified maintenance issues that created cascading problems. Stan and Tommy mapped the actual workflow versus the official workflow, showing dozens of places where workers had developed better methods that management didn't know about.

Jennifer, the youngest but perhaps the sharpest, saw the pattern first. "Look at this," she said, pointing to the various maps and charts. "Major problem traces back to communication failures. Quality doesn't talk to production.

Production doesn't talk to maintenance. Nobody talks to purchasing. We're not a factory, we're six different companies that happen to share a building."

"My great-grandmother said something similar," Tommy said quietly.

"About Hawthorne. She said the biggest change wasn't the lighting or the breaks. It was that suddenly everyone was paying attention to the same thing at the same time."

"The attention effect," Will said. "Mayo called it that. Not the Hawthorne Effect, that was what outsiders called it. Mayo knew it was about attention, about being seen and heard."

John thought about his desk on the factory floor, how it had changed the dynamic just by being there. Visibility. Presence. Attention.

"What if we didn't just fix the communication?" he said slowly. "What if we reorganized the entire flow of work and communication?"

They spent the afternoon redesigning Line 3, not the machines, but the human systems around them. Quality inspectors positioned where they could immediately give feedback to operators. Maintenance stationed at problem points instead of in a separate shop. Visual management boards that everyone could see and update.

"This is radical," Stefan said, running financial projections. "But the numbers work. Productivity would increase maybe twenty percent, but quality improvements and maintenance savings, we're looking at margin improvements of fifteen to eighteen percent."

"Morrison will never approve it," Bobby said.

"David Sterling might," John countered. "If we present it right."

As if summoned by his name, Sterling appeared in the doorway. The CEO was a small man, almost invisible in his gray suit and gray hair, but his eyes were sharp behind wire-rimmed glasses.

"Mr. Valerio," he said. "I hear you've been making changes." John's team tensed, but he stepped forward.

"Would you like to see what we're working on?" For the next hour, they walked Sterling through their analysis, their proposals, Stefan's real numbers. Sterling said nothing, just listened, occasionally nodding. Finally, he spoke.

"Harold Morrison has worked for my board for fifteen years. He has their complete confidence." He paused. "I, on the other hand, have been CEO for only two years, brought in to 'manage the transition.' Do you understand what that means?"

"They brought you in to shut us down," Rosa said bluntly.

Sterling smiled, the first time John had seen him do so. "They brought me in to make the numbers work for a sale. But they never specified what kind of numbers or what kind of sale." He looked at Stefan's laptop.

"These numbers, can you verify them?"

"Every penny," Stefan said.

"Then you have ninety days. Transform Line 3. Show me it works. Give me numbers even Morrison can't dispute." Sterling turned to leave, then paused.

"My father worked at Western Electric. In Kearny, not Chicago, but he knew about the Hawthorne experiments. He used to say management learned the wrong lesson. They thought it was about manipulating conditions to motivate workers. The real lesson was that workers are people, not machines. Treat them as people, and they'll surprise you."

After Sterling left, the team sat in stunned silence. Ninety days. It was both more and less time than they'd hoped for.

"We need help," Jennifer said. "We can't transform Line 3 by ourselves."

"No," John agreed. "We need everyone on Line 3 to be part of this." That afternoon, they called a meeting. Not a mandatory meeting, John specifically said anyone who didn't want to participate could continue their regular shift.

Everyone came anyway. Word had spread about Sterling's visit, about the ninety-day deadline. The workers of Line 3 gathered in a circle, forty-three people who collectively had over eight hundred years of experience at Meridian.

John stood in the center, feeling exposed. These weren't MBA students or management consultants. These were people whose livelihoods depended on what happened next.

"You all know me by now," he began. "Tony Valerio's grandson, the BIT kid who thinks he can fix things. And you're right to be skeptical. How many people like me have come through here with big ideas?" Murmurs of agreement, some bitter laughter.

"But here's what's different," John continued. "I'm not here to fix you. You're not the problem. You never were. The problem is that for decades, this company has ignored its greatest asset, your intelligence, your experience, your ideas." He pointed at Tommy.

"Tommy Kowalski suggested moving the inspection station a few inches. Defects dropped forty percent. That's not my success or management's success. That's Tommy's success, based on years of observation that no one bothered to ask about."

Rosa stood up. "What exactly are you proposing?" "I'm proposing we redesign Line 3 together. Every person here has ideas about how to do their job better. We implement those ideas. We document the improvements. We show the board that this plant's workers are worth investing in, not disposing of."

"And if Morrison blocks us?" someone called out.

"Then we go around him," John said. "We work weekends if we have to. We use our own time. Because this isn't just about saving jobs, it's about proving something that should never have needed proving: that the people doing the work know how to do it better than anyone else."

An older worker, Eddie Zawicki, raised his hand. "I've been here thirty-four years. You know how many times I've heard speeches like this?"

"How many?" John asked.

"Six. You're the seventh. But you're the first one who moved his desk to the floor. You're the first one who got his hands dirty moving that inspection station. So I'll give you something I've never given the others, the benefit of the doubt."

Eddie reached into his lunch pail, pulled out a notebook. "Years of improvements I never bothered suggesting because no one would listen. You want them? They're yours. But I want credit this time. My name on the improvements. My grandkids should know their grandfather wasn't just a pair of hands."

One by one, others pulled out notebooks, scraps of paper, drawings on napkins. The accumulated wisdom of Line 3, hidden in lunch pails and lockers, in heads and hearts.

Jennifer and Stefan set up a system to document everything. Bobby and his maintenance team started listing every modification they'd made unofficially to keep machines running. Rosa pulled out her quality data, twenty years of patterns that could predict and prevent defects.

By evening, they had over two hundred improvement suggestions, ranging from tiny adjustments to complete workflow redesigns.

"This is impossible," Stefan said, looking at the pile. "We can't implement all of these in ninety days."

"We don't have to," Tommy said. He'd been quiet most of the afternoon, but now he stood. "We start with small movements. The small stuff that makes the big stuff possible. My great-grandmother learned that at Hawthorne. Small changes, but everyone watching, everyone participating. The attention itself becomes part of the change."

John thought of Anna Kowalski in those photographs, her steady gaze, her hope that someone would finally listen. "Tommy's right. We start small. But we document everything. Every improvement, every result. We make it impossible to ignore."

• • •

That night, John drove to Solvay to meet Catherine Kowalski at the Polish nursing home. She was in the common room, a small woman wrapped in a crocheted shawl, her eyes the same sharp blue as Tommy's.

"So you're Tony Valerio's grandson," she said in accented English.

"Sit. Tell me what's happening at the plant." John described the workshop, the ninety-day deadline, the workers sharing their hidden improvements. Catherine listened, occasionally nodding.

"My mother died in 1962," she said when he finished. "But before she died, she told me about Hawthorne, about the experiments. You know what she said was the most important thing?"

"What?"

"That for six years, she mattered. Her opinion mattered. Her comfort mattered. Her ideas mattered. Even after the experiments ended, even after the Depression came and everything changed, she held onto that. The memory of mattering."

She pulled out a leather journal, its cover worn smooth. "My mother's diary. She wrote in Polish, but I translated parts." She opened it to a marked page. "This is from 1927, when that woman visited, Mary Follett."

She read: "Today a woman came who understood. Not like the men with their clipboards and theories. She asked real questions. She looked at us like we were people, not specimens. She said something I will remember forever: 'Power-with, not power-over.' Someday, she said, all factories will understand this. I hope I live to see it."

Catherine closed the journal, looked at John. "She didn't live to see it. Neither will I, probably. But maybe my grandson will. Maybe what you're doing is the beginning of what my mother hoped for." She handed him the journal.

"Take this. Show Tommy. Show the others. Let them know this isn't new, this idea that workers matter. It's old. It just keeps getting buried and having to be discovered again."

John drove back to the plant through dark streets, the journal on the seat beside him. The night shift was in full swing when he arrived, but Line 3 was different. Workers had already started implementing some of the simple improvements, repositioning tools, adjusting workflows, and adding visual markers. Small changes, small movements, but the difference was palpable.

He found Tommy at his station and showed him his great-grandmother's journal. Tommy read the translated passages, his hands still for once.

"She never told us she kept a diary," he said quietly. "My grandmother never mentioned it." "Maybe she was waiting for the right time," John suggested. "For when someone would understand what it meant." Rosa Washington approached, holding a clipboard.

"First shift's quality numbers," she said. "Best in years. And that's with just the tiny changes we made today. We are preventing errors from happening in the first place." Word spread through the plant. Workers from other lines drifted over to see what Line 3 was doing. Some scoffed, but others watched with interest. A few asked if they could suggest improvements for their own lines.

"I think this is how it spreads," Will Moffitt said, appearing beside John.

"Not through mandates or programs, but through attention. Through proof. Through hope."

Harold Morrison appeared at the end of the shift, his face tight with anger. "I hear you're making unauthorized changes."

"We're making improvements," John said calmly. "David Sterling approved a ninety-day pilot."

"I wasn't consulted."

"You weren't required."

Morrison stepped closer, lowering his voice. "You have no idea who you're dealing with. I have connections you can't imagine. I will bury you and your little experiment."

"Maybe," John said. "But you'll have to do it in front of everyone."

They're all watching now. It was true. The entire Line 3 crew had stopped to watch the confrontation. Morrison looked around, calculating, then retreated without another word.

"He'll sabotage us," Tommy said after Morrison left.

"Let him try," Rosa said. "I've got years of documentation. Stefan has five years of real numbers. We've got ninety days of attention focused on Line 3. Everyone's watching now, the workers, Sterling, even the board will be watching."

John thought of Mayo at Hawthorne, not fully understanding what he'd discovered. The productivity improvements hadn't come from better lighting or optimal break schedules. They'd come from attention itself, from being seen, from mattering.

Now Line 3 was under the spotlight. Every improvement would be documented. Every success would be visible. Every worker's contribution would be recognized.

"The attention effect," he said to himself, but Tommy heard him.

"My great-grandmother called it something else," Tommy said. "She called it dignity. The dignity of being treated as a thinking human being."

As the night shift ended and dawn broke over Onondaga Lake, John stood at his desk on the factory floor, surrounded by suggestions, improvements, possibilities. In ninety days, they would either transform Line 3 or Morrison would shut them down.

But something had already transformed. The workers were talking to each other across shifts, sharing ideas openly. The invisible walls between departments were becoming visible, and therefore breakable. The accumulated wisdom of decades was finally being spoken aloud.

John opened Anna Kowalski's journal to a page Catherine had marked: "The managers think we work harder because they're watching. They don't understand. We work harder because we're finally being seen."

"There's a difference between being watched and being seen. Being watched makes you careful. Being seen makes you matter."

He thought of his grandfather, demoted for seeing workers too clearly. Of Will Moffitt, keeping years of ignored suggestions. Of Rosa Washington, documenting quality problems no one wanted to acknowledge. They'd all been watching. Now, finally, someone was seeing.

The revolution wouldn't come from programs or initiatives. It would come from attention, sustained, respectful attention to the intelligence that had always existed on the factory floor.

Morrison was right to be afraid. Once workers remembered they mattered, they couldn't be made to forget again.

The ghost of Anna Kowalski was stirring at Meridian, seventy years after Hawthorne. And this time, everyone was paying attention.

LESSONS LEARNED

The Pattern of Betrayed Promises

Maria Santiago's filing cabinets, documenting decades of labor-management conflict, reveal a pattern that haunts organizational change: promises of participation exchanged for worker concessions, followed by management reneging on those promises. Trust, once broken, requires consistent action over time to rebuild.

Chris Argyris on Defensive Routines

Chris Argyris (1923-2013) identified organizational defensive routines, the policies and actions that prevent embarrassment or threat but also prevent learning. These routines are not personal failures but systemic patterns, embedded in organizational culture and reinforced by incentive structures.

Creating Value Connection

Creating Value emphasizes that sustainable transformation requires building trust at every level of the organization. This trust is not established through proclamations or programs but through consistent action over time, through kept promises, honored commitments, and genuine respect demonstrated daily.

Regarding quality: "Quality isn't a department or checklist, it's a culture. When you empower the people closest to the work to identify and solve problems, quality becomes everyone's job."

CHAPTER 4

The Six Inch Move that Changed Everything

"Standards should not be forced down from above but rather set by the production workers themselves." — *Taiichi Ohno*

The day of the first moves dawned cold and gray, typical January weather for Syracuse that matched the uncertainty John felt as he drove to the plant. Weeks of workshops had built momentum, generated ideas, created a cautious optimism among workers who had learned to distrust optimism. But this would be the real test, a physical change to the factory floor that would either prove the new approach could work or confirm every skeptic's worst fears.

Tommy Kowalski was already at the plant when John arrived, standing by the press that had become the focus of so much attention. The massive machine, capable of stamping metal with thirty tons of force, had occupied the same spot on the factory floor for twenty-three years.

Every worker who had ever operated it knew its quirks: the way the feed mechanism sometimes jammed, the blind spot that made it difficult to monitor the output tray, the extra steps required to move finished pieces to the next station.

"We calculated it last night," Tommy said. "If we move the press a few inches north, we eliminate the blind spot, reduce the walk distance to the next station by four feet, and this is the part that really matters, we can add a gravity feed to the output tray that eliminates the manual lifting entirely."

John studied the space, seeing what Tommy had seen through years of observation. The current placement made a kind of sense if you looked only at the machine itself, centered in its allocated space, squared to the building's grid, aesthetically symmetrical. But work didn't care about symmetry. Work cared about efficiency, about reducing wasted motion, about making each task as easy as possible for the human being who had to perform it thousands of times each day.

"A few inches," John repeated. "That's all it takes?"

"A few is all it's ever taken. But nobody ever asked us where the machine should go. The engineers placed it where it made sense on paper. We've been working around their mistake ever since."

The approval process for the move had been surprisingly quick, not because the bureaucracy had changed, but because John had learned to work around it. Instead of filing a formal facilities request, he had framed the change as a "pilot study" under his authority as operations improvement lead. Instead of waiting for maintenance to schedule the work, he had arranged for the press operators themselves to handle the relocation, with appropriate safety protocols in place.

It was, he knew, a calculated risk. If something went wrong, if the move damaged the equipment or injured a worker, the blame would fall squarely on him. But the alternative was worse: another good idea lost to bureaucratic delay, another promise broken, another reason for workers to stop believing that change was possible.

The actual move took less than two hours. A team of five workers, led by Tommy, used hydraulic jacks to lift the press, rollers to position it, and levels to ensure it was properly aligned. They worked with the confident efficiency of people who understood both the machinery and the physics involved, the same efficiency that had been ignored for twenty-three years while engineers and managers made decisions from offices that had never felt the vibration of a press or the strain of lifting metal.

When the press was repositioned and the power reconnected, Tommy ran the first test pieces himself. The difference was visible immediately: no more craning to see the output tray, no more extra steps to move finished pieces, no more lifting required.

"That's it," Rosa Washington said, watching from nearby. She had come to observe, unable to stay away from what might be a turning point in the plant's history. "Twenty-three years of unnecessary work, fixed in two hours by the people who actually do the job."

Word spread through the plant with the speed that only factory floor gossip can achieve. By lunch, workers from other lines were coming by to see the relocated press, to hear Tommy explain the improvement, to ask whether similar changes might be possible in their areas.

By the end of the shift, John had received seventeen requests for similar assessments, seventeen workers who had seen the move and recognized that, for the first time in memory, someone was actually listening and doing something.

It was, he realized, exactly what Mary Parker Follett had predicted decades earlier: that intelligence existed throughout the organization, waiting only for someone to ask, to listen, to act. The revolution she had glimpsed at Hawthorne was finally, tentatively, beginning to take root in another factory, another generation, another chance to prove that workers were more than just hands.

A few inches. That was all it had taken to change everything.

• • •

January 15, 1993. John would remember the date for the rest of his life, the way his grandfather remembered Pearl Harbor and his father remembered Kennedy's assassination. Some dates carved themselves into memory not through grand catastrophe but through small revolutions, the moment when impossible became inevitable.

The transformation of Line 3 had been running for nine months. They'd survived Morrison's sabotage attempts, Stefan's careful documentation protecting them each time the CFO tried to manipulate numbers. They'd implemented 127 workers' suggestions, reducing defects by sixty-eight percent, and improving productivity by thirty-four percent. The board was impressed enough to extend the pilot to other lines.

But success had bred its own complications. The plant was scheduled for a massive reorganization, a three-day shutdown where specialized rigging crews would rearrange equipment based on the workflow improvements the teams had designed. The cost: $300,000. The promised benefits: twenty percent improvement in overall efficiency, seven days faster delivery, quality issues reduced fifty percent from identification and resolution at the source.

John arrived at 4 AM that Friday, before even the maintenance crew. He needed to walk the floor alone, to see the new layout one more time before the riggers arrived. The machines stood silent in the darkness, waiting like sleeping giants for their repositioning. His grandfather's modified Cincinnati Mill had been moved to storage to make room for the new configuration, progress displacing history.

The lights came on in sections as Will Moffitt arrived earlier than usual. The old man moved slower these days, the forty-three years of climbing those stairs finally showing in his gait.

"Couldn't sleep either?" Will asked.

"Too much riding on this. If the reorganization doesn't deliver the promised improvements..." "Morrison wins," Will finished. "The board loses confidence, Sterling gets overruled, and Morrison's investment group swoops in like vultures."

They walked the floor together, Will pointing out where each machine would move, how the new flow would eliminate the walking waste, the waiting waste, the transport waste they'd identified. It was elegant on paper, revolutionary in scope.

"Your grandfather would be proud," Will said. "This is what he always envisioned, workers and management together, designing better ways."

The rigging crew arrived at 6 AM, twelve men with specialized equipment, hydraulic lifts, steel rollers, all the apparatus needed to move machines that weighed tons. Their foreman, a man from Buffalo named Mike Torelli, studied the plans with professional skepticism.

"This is ambitious," he said. "Three days might not be enough."

"It has to be," John replied. "We're back in production Monday morning."

The work began. Machines that had stood in the same spots for decades were lifted, shifted, rotated. Power lines were rerouted, compressed air lines reconfigured. The factory floor became a coordinated chaos of motion and noise.

Tommy Kowalski arrived for what would have been his regular shift, even though the line was shut down. So did Rosa Washington, Jennifer Chen, Bobby Santos. One by one, Line 3's workers appeared, unable to stay away while their workplace was transformed.

"We could help," Tommy suggested. "We know these machines better than anyone." Torelli shook his head. "Insurance liability. Only certified riggers can move and install the equipment. You folks need to stay clear."

So, the workers watched from the designated safe areas as strangers rearranged their world. John could see the frustration in their faces, their improvements being implemented by people who didn't understand why each change mattered.

By Friday evening, they'd completed about a third of the moves. The factory looked like a giant's game of chess mid-match, some pieces in new positions, others waiting for their turn. Torelli's crew departed with promises to return early Saturday.

Saturday morning brought lake-effect snow, heavy and relentless. Two riggers called out, unable to make it in from Buffalo. The remaining crew worked slower, more cautiously. By noon, they were behind schedule.

"We need to prioritize," Torelli told John. "We can't move everything. Pick the most critical repositioning."

John called an emergency meeting in the break room. Tommy, Rosa, Will, Jennifer, Stefan, and a dozen other workers gathered around the plans spread on the table.

"Line 3 is the priority," Rosa said. "If we can't show the improvements there, nothing else matters." They worked through the afternoon, identifying the essential moves versus the nice-to-haves. Outside, the snow storm continued, muffling the sounds of the rigging crew's work.

By Saturday evening, more bad news. A hydraulic lift had failed, a seal blown, fluid everywhere. Replacement parts wouldn't arrive until Monday.

"We're done," Torelli announced. "We've moved what we can with the remaining equipment. About seventy percent of your plan. Sorry, but that's the best we can do."

John looked at the floor. Machines stood in their new positions, but the careful choreography was incomplete. The workflow they'd designed was broken, compromised.

"It won't work like this," Jennifer said quietly, running calculations on her calculator. "The partial implementation actually makes things worse in some areas. We've created new bottlenecks."

Morrison appeared in the doorway, having somehow learned about the problems. His smile was thin, satisfied.

"I hear there are difficulties," he said. "The board will be disappointed. Three hundred thousand dollars for a partial implementation that might reduce efficiency? That's the kind of failure that forces immediate decisions about a plant's future." He left without waiting for a response, his message delivered.

The workers stood in small groups, staring at their half-transformed workplace. Three generations of accumulated hope, nine months of proven improvements, all potentially undone by a snowstorm and a blown hydraulic seal.

"We could fix it ourselves," Bobby Santos said suddenly. "I mean, we can't move the big machines, but we could adjust the smaller stuff. Workbenches, tool stations, inspection points."

"Insurance …" Torelli began.

Tommy interrupted. "This is our workplace. Our jobs. Our future."

John looked around the room at the faces of people who'd been ignored for decades, who'd finally been heard, and weren't about to lose that voice again.

"Torelli, you and your crew go home," John said. "What happens after you leave isn't your responsibility." The foreman studied John for a moment, then nodded. "We were never here past five o'clock. Whatever happens after that, we didn't see it."

As the rigging crew departed, the Meridian workers stood in the silent factory, snow falling past the windows, machines waiting in their incomplete positions.

"We can't move the big presses," Bobby said. "But we can move everything else safely. Reposition workstations, adjust conveyor angles, relocate tool cribs. All the six-inch movements that add up."

"That's dozens of adjustments," Stefan said. "We'd need most of the night."

"Then we better get started," Rosa said.

What followed was something John would struggle to describe years later: part barn raising, part ballet, part revolution. Workers who'd competed for overtime now cooperated ignoring that it was unpaid. First shift and second shift, day workers and night workers, young and old, all moving through the factory with shared purpose.

Tommy led a team adjusting workstation heights, simple changes that would reduce fatigue and improve precision. Rosa directed quality station repositioning, implementing years of observations. Jennifer and the younger engineers recalculated workflows in real-time, adjusting the plan for what could be moved versus what couldn't.

Stan Pomorski, sixty-seven years old, taught his nephew's generation tricks for moving light equipment with pipes and leverage that predated hydraulic lifts.

"My father showed me this," he said, demonstrating how to "walk" an assembly table. "His father showed him. Polish engineering, from before there were engineers."

The maintenance crew, led by Bobby, didn't just move equipment, they fixed problems that had been tolerated for years. Compressed air lines were shortened, electrical runs simplified, decades of jury-rigged solutions replaced with elegant fixes.

Around midnight, pizza appeared, ordered by David Sterling, who'd somehow heard about the spontaneous overnight effort. The CEO arrived at 1 AM, wearing jeans and a Syracuse University sweatshirt instead of his usual gray suit.

"Need another pair of hands?" he asked.

John almost said no because of liability, insurance, corporate protocol. Then he saw that Sterling was serious.

"Tommy's team needs help with the inspection station," John said.

And so the CEO of Meridian spent the early morning hours following Tommy Kowalski's directions, moving an inspection station until it aligned perfectly with the modified workflow.

At 3 AM, someone turned on the radio. Motown classics filled the factory, the Temptations, the Supremes, Marvin Gaye. Rosa Washington started singing along to "Ain't No Mountain High Enough," and soon others joined in. The factory became something John had never imagined, joyful.

Will Moffitt sat on a crate, too tired to work but unable to leave, watching with eyes that had seen four decades of factory life. "This is what Follett meant," he said to John. "Power-with, not power-over. Look at us, management and workers, salary and hourly, all distinction dissolved in common purpose and action."

As dawn approached, the work was nearly complete. Not the grand plan, but something perhaps more important, hundreds of small improvements, each suggested by workers, each implemented by workers, each one a small movement toward efficiency.

The crowning moment came at 5:47 AM. Tommy stood at his workstation, the same Station 7 his grandfather had worked, that John's grandfather had worked, and frowned.

"Something wrong?" John asked.

"This machine," Tommy said, indicating the main assembly press. "If it was turned six inches, I wouldn't have to walk that extra step. It would make my job easier."

The entire floor went quiet. Everyone knew they couldn't move the big press, it would require the rigging crew, permits, planning.

"How much would it save annually?" Jennifer asked, calculating quickly. "Based on current production rates... about eight thousand dollars."

"Eight thousand dollars," Morrison's voice cut through the silence.

He'd arrived unnoticed, his suit impeccable despite the early hour.

"You want to spend more money to move a machine six inches for eight thousand dollars annual savings?"

"It's not about the money," Tommy said quietly. "It's about being heard."

Morrison laughed, harsh and dismissive. "Being heard doesn't pay bills. Being heard doesn't satisfy shareholders."

John felt the deflation in the room, the joy curdling into familiar disappointment. Morrison was right, in his way. Six inches wouldn't transform the bottom line.

But then John remembered his grandfather's suggestion to move a machine slightly to save steps. Ignored for years.

"We're moving it," John said.

"With what?" Morrison demanded. "Your rigging crew is gone. Insurance won't..."

"We're moving it six inches," John repeated. "We know how to do it safely." He looked around the room at exhausted faces, at people who'd worked through the night without pay, without promise of reward, just for the hope that their workplace could be better.

"Stan," he called out. "You said your father knew how to move anything with pipes and leverage. Can we move this press six inches?"

Stan studied the machine, walked around it slowly, his movements deliberate despite his exhaustion.

"We'd need everyone," he said finally. "All of us, working together.

"This is insane," Morrison protested. "Sterling, you can't allow..."

"I don't see anything," Sterling said calmly. "I'm going to get coffee. I'll be back in an hour. Whatever I don't see, I can't stop."

He left, and after a moment's hesitation, Morrison followed, pulling out his phone, no doubt calling board members, lawyers, anyone who could stop this madness.

But it was too late. The workers were already moving, following Stan's directions. Pipes were positioned, leverage points calculated. Bobby's team disconnected power and air lines with practiced efficiency.

Jennifer and the engineers figured angles and forces.

"Everyone needs to push at exactly the same time," Stan instructed.

"Steady pressure, no jerking. The machine will resist, then suddenly give. When it gives, stop immediately." They arranged themselves around the press, John, even Will Moffitt putting his hands on the cold metal.

"On three," Stan counted. "One... two... three." They pushed. The machine didn't move.

"Again," Stan said. "Together. One... two... three." The press shifted, just barely, maybe an inch.

"Again."

Push by push, inch by inch, they moved the massive press. Not through mechanical advantage or hydraulic power, but through collective human effort. Six inches took twenty minutes, everyone working together.

When it was done, they stood back, sweating despite the cold, looking at what they'd accomplished. The press sat in its new position, six inches from where it had been for twenty years.

Tommy walked to his station, tested the new positioning. His movements flowed naturally now, no extra step, no wasted motion. He ran a test piece through, then another.

"My God," he said, loud enough for everyone to hear. "They actually listened to me."

The words hung in the air, echo of his reaction when they'd moved the inspection station nine months earlier, but deeper now, more significant. This wasn't management listening. This was everyone listening, everyone acting, everyone mattering.

Rosa Washington started to applaud. Then Bobby, then Jennifer, then everyone, applauding not for John or Sterling or any individual, but for themselves, for what they'd proven.

Morrison returned with three board members. They surveyed the factory floor, machines in new positions, workers exhausted but exhilarated, the CEO in jeans drinking coffee from a paper cup.

"What happened here?" board chairman Elizabeth Hartwell asked.

"Six inches," John said. "Six inches happened."

She looked confused, so Tommy explained. Not just about moving the press, but about his great-grandmother at Hawthorne, about his grandfather's ignored suggestions, about forty years of accumulated wisdom finally being heard.

"You're telling me," Hartwell said slowly, "that these workers gave up their weekend to implement their own improvements?"

"We didn't give up anything," Rosa said. "We took something back. Our dignity. Our intelligence. Our right to improve our own work."

Morrison tried one last attack. "This is chaos. Unauthorized changes, insurance violations, complete breakdown of management structure…"

"Mr. Morrison," Hartwell interrupted. "What I see is a workforce so committed they'll work without pay to improve efficiency. What I see is management finally listening to the people who actually do the work. What I see is the future of American manufacturing."

She turned to Sterling. "David, I want a full report on these improvements. Actual numbers, not Morrison's projections."

Then to John: "Mr. Valerio, I want a presentation to the full board next month. Bring workers with you. I want to hear their voices, not filtered through management speak."

As the board members left, Morrison lingering to shoot one last venomous look at John, the workers began to disperse. They were exhausted but somehow energized, moving with a different bearing, heads higher, steps more certain.

"Monday will tell," Will said to John. "When we start production, we'll see if all these moves add up to transformation." Monday came. First shift arrived to find their workplace transformed, not just physically but psychologically. Every improvement had a name attached, a small placard indicating whose idea it was.

The line started at 6 AM.

By 8 AM, it was clear something fundamental had changed. The work flowed like water finding its natural channel.

Defects dropped to near zero.

Productivity exceeded even their most optimistic projections.

Product was ready to ship faster than anyone had even thought.

By noon, workers from other lines were drifting over to see what was happening. The energy on Line 3 was different, focused but relaxed, efficient but human.

Stefan ran the real numbers hourly, barely believing what he was seeing.

"We're exceeding every metric," he told John. "Quality up, productivity up, faster delivery." That afternoon, John stood at his desk on the factory floor, now surrounded by other desks as more managers moved out of their offices.

He picked up the framed photo of his grandfather at his machine and walked to where the Cincinnati Mill had been placed in its new position of honor, visible to everyone entering the plant.

He set the photo next to the machine, then added a new placard: *Six inches can change everything. Transformation begins with listening.* In memory of all whose voices went unheard. In honor of all who finally spoke.

Tommy Kowalski read it, nodded. "My great-grandmother would have liked that," he said. Then, after a pause: "Your grandfather would have too."

Harold Morrison's investment group's takeover attempt was slowed by a board that suddenly saw value where Morrison had only seen costs. David Sterling promoted John to Vice President of Operations with a mandate to transform the entire plant.

But John would always mark the real transformation from that January morning when together workers moved a machine six inches because it mattered to one man. Not because of the savings, not because of the efficiency, but because after decades of silence, a worker's intelligence was finally recognized.

Years later, when John wrote about the transformation of Meridian, he would struggle to explain the significance of six inches to people who measured success in millions. How could he make them understand that revolutions don't always announce themselves with manifestos and dramatic gestures? Sometimes they happen one small adjustment at a time, one voice heard, one dignity restored.

But Tommy understood. Rosa understood. Every worker who'd pushed that press six inches understood.

The machine had moved, but more importantly, the immovable had moved, the assumption that workers were hands but not minds, the belief that intelligence flowed only from above, the century-old ghost of Frederick Taylor who saw humans as inefficient machines.

Six inches. Such a small distance to travel.

Such a long journey to get there.

Such a revolution when it finally moved.

Ask, Listen, Act!

LESSONS LEARNED

Small Changes, Big Impact

Tommy Kowalski's suggestion to move the press six inches seems trivial by management standards. Yet this small adjustment, multiplied across thousands of changes, produced measurable improvements. More importantly, it demonstrated something that no amount of speeches or programs could prove: that worker ideas would be implemented, that worker knowledge mattered, that someone was finally listening.

W. Edwards Deming on Continuous Improvement

Deming taught that quality improvement is not a destination but a journey, not a program but a philosophy. His concept of continuous improvement, adapted by Toyota into kaizen, emphasizes that small, incremental changes sustained over time produce results that dramatic interventions cannot achieve. The six-inch move embodies this principle: revolution through evolution, transformation through accumulation.

Creating Value Connection

Creating Value describes how sustainable improvement emerges from thousands of small changes suggested by workers who understand their jobs intimately. Management's role is not to generate these improvements but to create conditions where they can emerge naturally.

"Empowerment isn't a slogan, it's giving people the permission to act, the capability to solve, and the safety to try."

PART TWO: BREAKING THE PATTERN
1993-1994

CHAPTER 5

The Workshops Begin

"A one-week kaizen (workshop) will get you more improvement than six months of studying the problem in a conference room." — Art Byrne

Spring arrived slowly in Syracuse, the gray of winter giving way to a tentative green that seemed uncertain of its welcome. Inside Meridian Manufacturing, a different kind of spring was emerging, a flowering of ideas that had been dormant for years, waiting only for the right conditions to bloom.

The success of the six-inch move had done what no amount of promises or presentations could achieve: it had demonstrated, in concrete and measurable terms, that worker ideas could be implemented and that implementation made a real difference. The productivity improvement on Tommy's station was documented at fourteen percent, not through working harder or faster, but through eliminating the unnecessary effort that had been built into the process for over two decades.

More importantly, the improvement was visible. Every worker who passed that station could see the change, could understand the logic behind it, could imagine similar changes in their own areas. The skepticism that had greeted John's first workshops began to give way to cautious engagement. Workers who had dismissed the initiative as another management fad started attending sessions, contributing ideas, allowing themselves to hope.

John expanded the workshop program methodically, understanding that sustainable change required a system rather than heroics. Each workshop followed a consistent format: workers identified problems, analyzed root causes, proposed solutions, tested, and developed implementation plans.

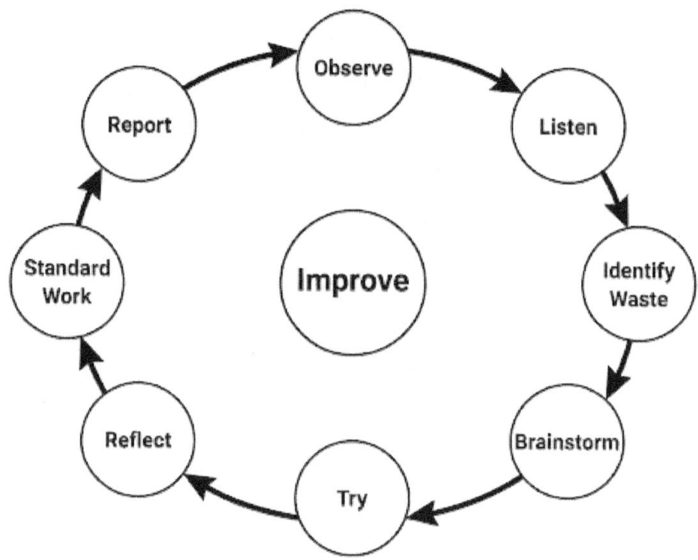

Workshop sign in the War Room

Management's role was to remove obstacles, provide resources, and, most critically, get out of the way when workers knew better than they did.

The results accumulated like compound interest, each improvement building on those that came before. A reorganization of the tool crib reduced search time by sixty percent. A redesign of the shift handoff process eliminated the communication gaps that had been causing quality defects. A worker-designed training program cut the learning curve for new employees by three weeks.

But the most significant change was invisible, measured not in productivity metrics but in the faces of workers who had regained their dignity through being heard. Tommy Kowalski, once the plant's most vocal skeptic, became its most passionate advocate, leading workshops in his area with the natural authority of someone who had earned respect through decades of excellent work.

"You know what's different?" he asked John one evening, after a particularly successful session. "It's not that we're doing anything new. We've always known how to improve things. What's different is that someone finally asked us, finally listened, finally let us try."

It was, John realized, the same observation Anna Kowalski had made at Hawthorne seventy years earlier, the same truth that had echoed through generations of workers waiting for their wisdom to be valued. Nothing had changed except the willingness to ask. Everything had changed because someone finally did.

• • •

The success of the six-inch movement had rippled through Meridian like electricity through water. Three months later, the transformation was no longer a question of whether but how fast, how far, how deep the changes could go. Harold Morrison fought a rearguard action from his executive office, but his power was waning like winter ice in April sun.

The workshop methodology that John and Will Moffitt had refined was about to be tested at scale. Twenty-five workshops planned for the year, an ambitious goal that would require fundamentally reimagining how work stopped and started, how problems were solved, and how knowledge moved through the organization.

But before the first workshop invitation was posted, Will Moffitt raised the question that would define everything that followed.

They were in Will's office, the one he rarely used, now preferring the floor. John had drafted the workshop schedule, the team selections, and the methodology outline. Will studied it all with the careful attention of a man who had seen forty years of improvement initiatives bloom and wither.

"You're missing the most important thing," Will said finally.

"What?"

"The promise. The one that matters more than all the rest."

John waited.

"No one loses their job because of improvement." Will set down the papers. "Think about it, John. You're about to ask workers to study their own jobs and find ways to do them better, faster, and with less effort. You're asking them to eliminate waste. Do you know what waste looks like to a worker who's been through three rounds of layoffs? Waste looks like their neighbor's job. Waste looks like their own job."

The words landed hard. John had been so focused on methodology, on the mechanics of observation and analysis and implementation, that he'd missed the fundamental human calculus at the heart of every improvement effort. Why would any sane person help make their work more efficient if the reward for efficiency was a pink slip?

"I watched it happen at a great company in the eighties," Will continued. "They called it Work-Out. Beautiful program, genuinely empowering. Workers came up with ideas that saved millions. And then the layoffs came anyway. Not because of the improvements, the layoffs were coming regardless, but the workers didn't know that. All they knew was that they'd made themselves more productive and then people got let go. The message was devastating: your ideas are the rope they'll hang you with."

Will leaned forward. "The Japanese understood this instinctively. Toyota never laid off workers for making improvements. When a team found a way to do the same work with fewer people, those freed-up workers didn't get fired. They got redeployed. They went to new lines, joined improvement teams, trained others, supported growth. The productivity gains were captured through attrition and expansion, not through elimination."

"Accounting would have…"

"Accounting would have taken every efficiency gain and converted it to headcount reduction. That's what financial engineers do. They see a freed-up worker and they see a cost to cut. They never see a freed-up worker as capacity for growth, or as a teacher who can spread the improvement to the next line, or as a problem-solver who can tackle the backlog of issues no one's had time to address."

John thought of Tommy's story about the safety team. How he'd identified seventeen hazards, fixed them all, and then watched his colleagues get laid off six months later. The lesson every worker at Meridian had internalized: don't make yourself dispensable. Don't improve yourself out of a job. Don't hand management the efficiency study that becomes the justification for the next reduction in force.

It was the invisible wall that no methodology could breach. You could teach people the tools of improvement. You could show them the data. You could even convince them that management was sincere. But if the historical pattern said that productivity gains led to layoffs, no amount of sincerity would overcome the evidence of experience.

"So what do we do?" John asked.

"You make the pledge. Publicly. Unequivocally. No one will lose their job as a result of improvement. Period. Not repositioned against their will, not transferred to a worse assignment, not placed on a list for the next downturn. If workshops free up capacity, that capacity goes to supporting growth, filling natural attrition, staffing new lines, joining the improvement teams themselves. The gains get captured, but not on the backs of the people who created them."

"Can we keep that promise?"

Will fixed him with a look that carried decades of hard-won wisdom. "You have to. Because if you make it and break it, you won't just destroy this initiative. You'll destroy the possibility of any initiative, for a generation. Workers have long memories, John. They remember every broken promise, every betrayal, every time management said, 'trust us' and then proved unworthy of that trust. One layoff after an improvement event and you'll never get another honest idea from this floor."

John brought it to Sterling the next morning. The CEO listened, then nodded slowly.

"My father told me something about the Hawthorne works," Sterling said. "When the experiments ended and the

Depression hit, Western Electric laid off thousands. The women from the relay assembly room, the ones who'd given everything to those experiments, most of them were let go. The company got years of groundbreaking research from their participation and rewarded them with unemployment. My father said that story traveled through every factory in America. It taught a whole generation of workers that cooperation with management was a sucker's bet."

Sterling picked up a pen. "Write the policy. I'll sign it. No layoffs resulting from improvement activities. Freed-up capacity goes to growth, attrition, training, or new improvement work. We capture the gains through patience, not through cuts."

The announcement went up on every bulletin board in the plant the following Monday, signed by Sterling, countersigned by the union president. John watched the workers read it, watched their faces cycle through disbelief, skepticism, and finally a cautious, fragile willingness to consider that this time might be different.

Tommy Kowalski read it twice, then looked at John. "Words on paper. We'll see."

"Yes," John said. "You will."

It would take months before the pledge was tested, and years before it was truly believed. But it changed the fundamental equation of every workshop that followed. When workers sat down to study their processes, they weren't calculating whether their honesty might cost a colleague's livelihood. They were free to see waste as waste, inefficiency as inefficiency, and opportunity as opportunity, without the terrible arithmetic of self-preservation corrupting every observation.

The freed-up workers became the transformation's most powerful asset. As improvements reduced the labor needed on one line, those experienced workers carried their knowledge to the next line, and the next. They became teachers, facilitators, and problem-solvers. The capacity that Accounting would have eliminated became the engine that accelerated change across the entire plant.

It was, Will told John later, the single most important decision of the entire transformation. Not the six-inch move, not the workshops, not the data or the methodology. The promise that improvement would never be used as a weapon against the people who created it. Without that promise, none of the rest would have been possible.

• • •

The first formal workshop began on a Monday morning that smelled of lilacs blooming in the abandoned lot next door, their sweetness mixing incongruously with machine oil and metal. The team assembled in what they now called the War Room with its brown paper walls covered in workflows, data, and photographs from the recent workshops.

This workshop would focus on Line 2, the stamping operation that fed components to Line 3. Seven people gathered around the scarred wooden table: Rosa Martinez from first shift, Michael Williams from second shift, Young Park from engineering, Dianne Foster from purchasing, Joey Torretti from maintenance, Angela Kowalski, Tommy's daughter, fresh from Syracuse University, and surprisingly, Father Patrick O'Brien from St. Brigid's, where most of the Polish and Italian workers attended mass.

"Why a priest?" Morrison had demanded when he saw the roster.

"Because he's worked the line," John had replied. "Summers during seminary, full time for two years when the diocese couldn't afford to pay him. He knows stamping better than our engineers."

Father Pat, as the workers called him, still had the hands to prove it, scarred, thick-fingered, one nail permanently blackened from a press accident in 1987.

"We begin with observation," Will Moffitt explained, leading the session. At seventy-one, he moved with the dignified care of someone preserving energy for important moments. "Not judgment, not solutions, just watching. What actually happens versus what we think happens."

They spent the entire first morning on the floor, watching Line 2 operate. No clipboards initially, no timing, just observation. Rosa pointed out how operators had to twist to reach controls, a movement so smooth it looked natural but was over time wearing out shoulders and backs. Michael showed how second shift had developed different methods than first shift, neither knowing about the other's innovations.

"My father did this job for thirty years," Joey said, watching the press operator dance between stations. "Retired with a spine like a question mark. Never occurred to anyone to move the controls to where the operator stands."

Young Park, the engineer, was sketching constantly.

"The original design assumed operators would stand here," he pointed to a spot no one used. "But the sight lines are wrong. You can't see the material feed from there."

"We figured that out before," Rosa said dryly. "Told three different engineers. They said we were standing in the wrong place."

Father Pat laughed, a sound that filled the floor. "The eternal argument, are the workers doing it wrong, or is the design wrong? As if the work and the worker could be separated."

Angela Kowalski was documenting everything with a video camera, a new addition to their methodology. "My great-grandmother would have loved this," she said. "We get to record how work is done, not just the output."

That afternoon, they began mapping the current state. Not the official process, but what really happened. The brown paper soon filled with sticky notes, each one a task, a decision, a workaround that had evolved over decades.

"Look at this," Dianne Foster said, tracing the material flow. "Purchasing buys steel based on a forecast that production never sees. Production schedules based on customer orders that purchasing doesn't track. We're two companies that happen to share a building."

"Three companies," Michael corrected. "First shift, second shift, and weekend crew. We don't even use the same setup procedures."

The revelation came Tuesday morning. Young Park had spent the night analyzing the workflow maps, and he arrived with dark circles under his eyes but excitement in his voice.

"We're not running a production line," he announced. "We're running three different production lines on the same equipment. Each shift has optimized for their own reality, but the optimizations conflict."

He spread out drawings, showing how each shift's methods made sense in isolation but created chaos in transition. First shift optimized for quality. Second shift for speed. The weekend crew adjusted for minimal staffing.

"It's like a marriage where the spouses never talk," Father Pat observed. "Each doing their best but working at cross purposes."

The solution began to emerge through what Will called "circular response", Follett's term for how ideas build on each other in groups.

Rosa suggested standardizing the best practices from each shift. Michael proposed overlapping crews to transfer knowledge. Joey identified equipment modifications that would make the standard practices physically easier.

But the breakthrough came from Angela, youngest in the room, carrying the weight of the Kowalski legacy.

"What if we stop thinking about shifts and start thinking about the product?" she said. "The metal doesn't care what time it is. The press doesn't know if it's Tuesday or Saturday. What if we organized around the work itself, not the schedule?"

The room went quiet, processing the implications. It would mean restructuring years of labor agreements, shift differentials, and supervisor hierarchies.

"The union would never..." someone started.

"The union would love it," Father Pat interrupted. "If it meant workers had more control over their process, more dignity in their work. The union isn't against change, it's against change that diminishes workers."

They spent Wednesday designing the new system. Not three shifts but three teams, each responsible for a complete product family, overlapping to share knowledge and maintain continuity. The same equipment, but used differently, like a piano played by jazz musicians instead of classical, same keys but different music.

Stefan Pomorski joined them to run the numbers. "This is radical," he said, his ThinkPad heating from the calculations. "But if it works...Thirty percent productivity improvement, fifty percent reduction in transition losses, and actually lower overtime costs because people won't be fixing other shift's problems."

"Morrison will kill it," Dianne said.

"Morrison's leaving," David Sterling announced from the doorway. None of them had heard him arrive.

"The board met this morning. He is giving up his CFO role but will remain on the Board. Stefan, you're interim CFO." Stefan's laptop slipped from his fingers, caught at the last second by Joey. "I'm... what?"

"You're the only one who understands the real numbers," Sterling said. "The only one the workers trust with the books. The board agrees."

The workshop took on new energy. Without Morrison's shadow, ideas flowed freely. They designed visual management systems, boards that would show every worker every metric in real-time. No hidden numbers, no manipulated reports.

"Transparency," Will Moffitt said. "Follett argued for it in the 1920s. When everyone sees the same information, power equalizes."

Thursday brought implementation planning. They would pilot the new system on one press, volunteers only. If it worked, it would spread naturally without mandates or forced compliance.

"Like yeast," Father Pat said. "You don't have to put it everywhere. Put it in one place and it spreads on its own."

Rosa volunteered her press first. "Twenty-three years on that machine. If anyone's going to prove this works, it should be someone who knows every sound it makes."

Michael immediately volunteered to partner with her, second shift learning from first, first shift learning from second. Within an hour, they had twelve volunteers, enough for a complete pilot.

The physical changes began Thursday afternoon. Small movements, controls relocated, seats adjusted, tool positions optimized. Each change had a name attached, honoring the suggester. Rosa's reach reduction. Michael's sight line improvement. Joey's maintenance access panel.

Word spread through the plant. Workers from other lines drifted over to watch. They asked questions and made suggestions. The workshop boundaries became permeable, anyone could contribute, and every idea was documented.

"This is what we missed before," Will told John, watching the organic spread of involvement. "We thought workshops were events. They're not. They're punctuation marks in an ongoing conversation."

Friday morning, the pilot began. Rosa started the press with Michael beside her, both of them learning the hybrid method they'd developed.

The first pieces were slow, awkward. By noon, they'd found their rhythm. By end of shift, they were exceeding both previous shifts best numbers.

"It's not faster," Rosa explained to the gathered crowd. "It's smoother. Like the difference between rushing and flowing." Angela's video captured something remarkable, Rosa and Michael teaching each other simultaneously, decades of accumulated knowledge transferring in real-time. Her precision with his efficiency, his shortcuts with her quality consciousness.

"My dad needs to see this," Angela said. "Tommy Kowalski needs to see his daughter carrying on Anna's legacy, but different, not just being heard, but facilitating others being heard." The workshop officially ended Friday at 3 PM, but the work continued.

Weekend crew joined the experiment, adding their innovations. Their techniques developed for skeleton staffing that improved safety and quality when fully staffed.

Stefan worked through the weekend, documenting the impact. "It's not just the productivity," he explained to Sterling and the board members who'd come to see. "It's the reduction in errors, rework, overtime fixes. We're saving money we didn't even know we were spending."

Monday morning brought validation. The pilot press ran all day without a single defect, exceeding quota by twenty percent while using less raw material. Rosa's precision reduced waste that had been accepted as normal for decades.

Other presses wanted in. By Wednesday, half of Line 2 had adopted variations of the new method. Not because they were told to, but because they saw it working and adapted it to their own needs.

"This is the difference," John explained to Elizabeth Hartwell when she visited. "Previous initiatives failed because they were imposed. This is emerging. Workers are choosing to change because they're designing the change."

Hartwell watched Rosa training a new employee, using Angela's video to show both old and new methods, explaining why the changes mattered.

"My grandfather competed with Meridian for sixty years," Hartwell said. "He always said you had the best workers in Syracuse, possibly in America. But he also said you'd never beat us because you didn't trust them. Looks like that's finally changing."

• • •

The next workshop, focusing on maintenance, began two weeks later. Bobby Santos led it, bringing together mechanics from all shifts, operators who did their own adjustments, and engineers who'd designed equipment they'd never maintained.

"Every machine tells a story," Bobby said, leading them through the mechanical forest of Line 1. "This press here, see the welded reinforcement? That's from 1987 when we were running double shifts and it started cracking. No money for replacement, so we fixed it. Been running better ever since. But engineering doesn't know about it, so the drawings are wrong, the spare parts don't fit, and every new mechanic has to learn the hard way." They documented every modification, every work-around, every tribal knowledge that existed only in mechanics' heads. The young engineers were horrified and fascinated in equal measure.

"We've been designing improvements for equipment that doesn't exist," one admitted. "The machines on our drawings versus the machines on the floor, they're cousins, not twins."

Father Pat, who'd joined this workshop too, offered theological perspective. "It's like the difference between doctrine and faith. The official version versus the lived experience. Both true, neither complete without the other."

The maintenance workshop produced something unexpected, a complete equipment genealogy, showing how machines had evolved through worker modifications over decades. It was a history of intelligence applied at the point of work, mostly undocumented, entirely uncredited.

"This is our real asset," Sterling told the board. "Not the equipment, but the accumulated knowledge of how to make it work better than designed. Like making moonshine." By the third workshop, focused on quality, Rosa Washington finally got her moment. Twenty years of data, patterns she'd tracked that no one had wanted to see.

"Every defect has a signature," she explained, her quiet voice commanding attention. "Monday morning defects are different from Friday afternoon defects. Winter defects are different from summer. First piece defects are different from last piece. I know them all."

She taught the workshop to read defects like text, each one telling a story about what went wrong and why. The engineers were astounded; Rosa had developed a diagnostic system more sophisticated than anything in their textbooks.

"Why didn't you ever…" someone began.

"I tried," Rosa said simply. "Nineteen seventy-eight. Nineteen eighty-three. Nineteen eighty-seven. Nineteen ninety-one. I tried. No one listened. So I kept tracking, hoping someday someone would."

The quality workshop revolutionized inspection. Instead of checking finished products, they implemented Rosa's predictive system, knowing when and where defects were likely, *preventing* rather than detecting.

"It's like weather forecasting," Rosa explained. "You don't wait for rain to know you need an umbrella. You read the signs."

By summer, the workshop rhythm was established. Every two weeks, a cross-functional team would tackle a specific problem. Not in conference rooms but on the floor, not in theory but in practice.

The workshops became events that workers looked forward to. Being selected for one was an honor. The ideas generated were implemented immediately, with full credit to the suggester. The walls of the War Room filled with success stories, each with names and photos attached.

"We're creating a different culture," Will Moffitt reflected, watching a workshop where the newest hire was teaching veteran workers a technique he'd learned in community college. "Not top-down or bottom-up, but circular, flowing in all directions."

John thought of Anna Kowalski at Hawthorne, being observed but not included in the analysis. Now her great-great-granddaughter was facilitating workshops where workers analyzed themselves, designed their own improvements, implemented their own ideas.

"The revolution is complete when it doesn't need leaders," Father Pat observed during a break. "When the system itself generates continuous improvement, continuous respect, continuous dignity."

But the real measure of success came from an unexpected source. A delegation from Japan, having heard about the transformation, visited.

They spent three days observing, asking questions, and taking notes.

"You've done something we struggle with," their lead engineer admitted to John. "You've made American workers embrace continuous improvement not as a Japanese import but as their own idea. You've made it cultural, not procedural."

Tommy Kowalski, showing them his line, smiled at the irony. "You learned from us in the fifties when you visited. We're just finally learning from ourselves." The workshop program would eventually transform every aspect of Meridian, but its real impact was deeper. It proved that workers had always been capable of redesigning their work, they'd just never been invited to do so.

Each workshop was a small revolution, a quiet assertion that intelligence existed at every level, that dignity meant the right to improve one's own work, that power-with created value that power-over could never achieve.

Mary Parker Follett had written about circular response, how ideas in groups build on each other in ways that transcend individual contribution. Seventy years later, in a Syracuse factory, her theory was becoming practice.

The workshops would continue, evolve, and spread to other companies. But their genesis, that first formal gathering of seven workers around a table, treating each other as equals regardless of title or tenure, that was the moment when transformation became systematic rather than sporadic.

• • •

Stefan Kowalski chose to work the night hours, preferring the relative solitude to the bustle of day shifts. He was Tommy's cousin, another branch of the family tree that connected Syracuse to Chicago, to Hawthorne, to the origins of everything they were trying to accomplish.

But where Tommy was vocal and confrontational, Stefan was quiet and observant, accumulating wisdom through patient attention rather than passionate argument.

"The night shift sees things differently," Stefan told John during one of these late-night visits, his voice barely audible above the press of machinery.

The night shift operated in a different world, quieter in some ways, louder in others, with shadows pooling between the overhead lights and the steady rhythm of machines creating a cathedral-like atmosphere that day workers rarely experienced. John had begun coming in for night observations at Will's suggestion, understanding that the factory's third shift often harbored both the most experienced workers and the most neglected problems.

"We have time to watch, to think, to notice patterns that get lost in the rush of daylight," Stefan continued. "Things that should be fixed but never are. Problems that everyone knows about, but no one mentions."

He led John to a station near the back of Line 3, where a worker named Roberto was wrestling with a stubborn mechanism that seemed designed to resist human effort. The task should have taken thirty seconds; Roberto spent nearly two minutes on each piece, fighting against a design that worked in theory but failed in practice.

"How long has this been a problem?" John asked.

Stefan's laugh was quiet but telling. "Since before I started here, which means at least fifteen years. Everyone who works this station knows it's broken. Everyone has ideas about how to fix it. But no one's ever asked, and the workers who tried to say something anyway got told to stop complaining and do their jobs." Roberto looked up, his expression caught between wariness and hope.

"You're the one from BIT? The one who moved the press?"

"I'm the one who asked the workers who moved the press."

The distinction seemed to matter. Roberto's posture shifted, becoming more open, more willing to engage. "This mechanism... it's supposed to engage automatically, but the tolerance is wrong. The engineers designed it based on new parts, but after a few months of use, the wear changes everything. We end up fighting it every time."

"What would fix it?"

Roberto hesitated, years of being ignored battling against the possibility that this time might be different.

"A spring. A stronger spring in the return mechanism. Maybe three dollars worth of parts, fifteen minutes of installation. But we'd need a work order, and the work order would need engineering approval, and engineering would need to do a study, and..."

"And the study would take months and conclude that the cost of fixing it exceeded the cost of living with it and it would probably cause other problems," John finished.

"You've done this before."

"I've seen the pattern. But I'm trying to break it."

The spring was installed the following week, after John circumvented the approval process with the same "pilot study" authority that had enabled the press move. The productivity improvement was modest, perhaps eight percent, but the symbolic impact was enormous.

Word spread through the night shift that someone had, at long last, gone and seen the problem, asked questions, listened, acted, and finally fixed a problem that had been ignored for over a decade.

Within a month, John had received suggestions from night shift workers that exceeded the combined total from the previous five years. The third shift, long neglected and longer ignored, had become the transformation's most enthusiastic participant.

The transformation had found its rhythm.

Six-inch moves had become the rallying cry.

And every workshop began with the same principles: We are here to observe, ask questions and listen to each other.

Because being heard, it turned out, was the beginning of everything.

LESSONS LEARNED

Structure That Enables Emergence

The workshop methodology provides structure without imposing outcomes. Workers identify problems, analyze root causes, propose solutions, and develop implementation plans. Management's role is to remove obstacles, provide resources, and get out of the way when workers know better.

Follett's Circular Response

Mary Parker Follett described 'circular response,' where each participant's contribution builds on others', creating solutions that no individual could have imagined alone. The workshops embody this principle: ideas building on ideas, knowledge integrating with knowledge, creating emergent solutions that represent collective wisdom.

Creating Value Connection

Creating Value describes the workshop as a technology for unlocking collective intelligence. The specific techniques matter less than the underlying principle: create conditions where workers feel safe contributing, where their ideas receive genuine consideration, where learning and implementation follows naturally from inclusion.

"Prioritize learning as a fundamental source of continuous improvement. The companies that sustain improvement are the ones that have built learning into the daily rhythm of work."

CHAPTER 6

Inclusion

"Empowerment is not giving people power, they already have it. Empowerment is creating conditions where people can use the power they already possess."

— Creating Value, (Wiley, 2025)

Three months after the six-inch move, John sat in the break room with Will Moffitt, watching the second shift arrive. The transformation was visible in ways that metrics couldn't capture: the pace of movement, the sound of conversation, the absence of the heavy silence that had greeted him on that first January morning.

"You've done something here," Will said, stirring his coffee with the deliberate movements of a man who had learned patience through decades of waiting for things to change. "But I want to make sure we understand what it means."

John looked up from the production reports Rosa had compiled. "We've improved productivity by eighteen percent. Quality defects are down sixty percent. On-time delivery..."

"Numbers." Will waved his hand dismissively. "I could get those numbers by cracking the whip harder. Morrison did it for years. Works for about six months, then everything falls apart worse than before. What we've done is different. But do you know why it's different?"

John considered the question. He had been so focused on the mechanics of the workshops, on tracking improvements and building momentum, that he hadn't stopped to articulate the underlying philosophy. "Because we're listening to the workers?"

"Closer. But not quite." Will leaned forward, his weathered hands wrapped around the coffee cup. "Tell me what happened yesterday in Cell 7."

"The bearing issue? Stefan identified that the supplier had changed specifications without telling anyone. He caught it before we shipped defective products to three major customers."

"And what would have happened six months ago?"

John thought about it. "Stefan would have noticed. He's been running that machine for twelve years, he notices everything. But he probably wouldn't have said anything. Or if he did, it would have gone through three layers of approval, gotten stuck in someone's inbox, and the defective product would have shipped anyway."

"Exactly. So what changed?"

"He has authority now. He can stop the line."

Will smiled, the deep creases around his eyes folding into something like satisfaction. "Now we're getting somewhere. But it's more than that. Think about what 'authority' really means in this context."

That conversation stayed with John through the rest of the week. He found himself watching more closely during the workshops, trying to understand not just what was happening but why.

On Thursday, Maria Santiago pulled him aside after a particularly productive session. "The CFO cornered me this morning," she said, her voice carrying the careful neutrality of someone navigating between factions. "He wanted to know why the union is cooperating with management's latest scheme to extract more labor for the same pay."

"I told him that for the first time in twenty years, my members feel like they have a voice in how they do their jobs. That's not extraction. That's the opposite of extraction."

"And he said?"

Maria's expression hardened. "He said that 'empowerment' is just a slogan for getting workers to do management's thinking for free. That we're being manipulated into giving away our leverage."

John had heard variations of this critique during his doctoral research, from union skeptics, from academic critics, from executives who dismissed the whole approach as naive. The accusation stung because it touched on something real. Wasn't he, in fact, asking workers to solve problems that management had created? Wasn't the company benefiting from their ideas without fundamentally changing the power structure?

"Do you believe that?" he asked Maria.

She was silent for a long moment. "I believe," she said finally, "that my father worked at a factory for thirty-two years. Brilliant man, could troubleshoot any machine on the floor, could see problems before they happened. And in all those years, nobody ever asked him what he thought. Not once. He retired feeling like he'd spent his life being invisible."

"I'm sorry."

"Don't be sorry. Be different." Maria's eyes met his with an intensity that made him want to look away.

"What you're doing here, it's not empowerment because you call it that, or because you have workshops and flip charts and improvement metrics. It's empowerment if, and only if, it actually changes what power means in this building."

The next morning, John arrived at the plant early and found Tommy Kowalski already at his station, adjusting the machine that had moved six inches and changed everything.

"Got a minute?" John asked.

Tommy glanced up, his expression guarded. Despite three months of successful collaboration, the wariness never entirely left his eyes, the residue of decades spent being ignored. "What do you need?"

"I need you to explain something to me. When we moved that machine six inches, what did that mean to you?"

Tommy stopped his adjustments, turning to face John fully for the first time. "You asking as a manager, or are you actually asking?"

"I'm asking."

Tommy was quiet for a moment, his hands still resting on the machine's controls. "Eighteen months," he said finally. "That's how long I'd been telling people that machine needed to move. I told my supervisor. Told his supervisor. Filled out suggestion forms. Brought it up in two 'safety awareness' meetings."

He pronounced the phrase with audible quotation marks. "Nothing. Not even a 'we'll look into it.' Just nothing."

"I remember you telling me. In our first workshop." "What you don't know is what happened after that first time I suggested it. The CFO called me into his office. Told me that machine placement decisions were 'above my pay grade.' That I should 'focus on doing my job' and leave the thinking to people with engineering degrees."

Tommy's jaw tightened at the memory. "I've got a two-year associate's degree in machine tooling and thirty-four years of experience. But I'm not supposed to have opinions about my own work. So when I requested the move you didn't just move a machine. You treated me like a human being with a functioning brain."

Tommy's voice carried something John hadn't heard before, not anger, but a kind of raw honesty that the plant's culture usually suppressed. "You know how rare that is? In thirty-four years, I can count on one hand the number of times a manager actually listened to something I said and then did something about it."

John thought about Maria's father, about all the accumulated wisdom that companies systematically waste. "That's not empowerment," he said slowly, working through the idea as he spoke. "That's just basic respect."

Tommy shook his head. "That's where you're wrong. Respect is the foundation, but it's not the building. What you did was give me something I hadn't had in decades: the ability to change something about my own work. Not suggest a change and hope someone approves it. Actually, change it."

Will found John that afternoon, staring at a whiteboard covered with workshop schedules and improvement metrics.

"You've got that look," Will said. "The one that says you're finally understanding something important."

"The CFO called what we're doing pseudo-empowerment." John said. "Getting workers to do management's thinking without actually giving them any power."

"And?"

"And I'm trying to figure out whether he's right."

Will pulled up a chair, settling into it with the deliberate movements of a man who had learned patience through decades of waiting for things to change. "Let me tell you about the three kinds of empowerment I've seen in forty years."

"The first kind is empowerment theater. Companies announce, 'empowerment initiatives,' hand out coffee mugs and posters, tell workers they're empowered, but nothing changes. Decisions still flow from the top-down. Suggestions still disappear into bureaucratic black holes. The only thing that's different is the vocabulary."

"That's what we had before," John said.

"That's what most companies have. It's comfortable for management because nothing has to change. You get to feel good about 'empowering' people without actually giving up any control."

"And the second kind?"

"Delegation disguised as empowerment. Management identifies problems, develops solutions, and then 'empowers' workers to implement those solutions. The workers have authority to execute, but not to think. They're empowered to follow instructions more autonomously."

John winced. "That's uncomfortably close to some of what we've done."

"Honest of you to admit it. The temptation is always there to use the language of empowerment while keeping the substance of control. But here's the thing: delegation isn't inherently bad. Sometimes workers do need to implement solutions that come from elsewhere. The problem is when that's all empowerment means."

"So what's the third kind?"

Will leaned forward, his voice taking on the intensity John had come to recognize as signaling something important.

"Real empowerment means giving people authority, capability, and support to make decisions about their own work. Not just to suggest improvements and hope they're approved. Not just to implement solutions that came from above. Making real decisions, with real consequences, within their areas of responsibility."

"That sounds like chaos."

"It sounds like chaos to people who've only known control. But think about Stefan yesterday. He didn't ask permission to stop the line when he found the bearing issue. He didn't fill out a form and wait for approval. He made a decision, the right decision I might add, and acted on it. That's empowerment."

"But he couldn't do that if…"

"If he didn't know how to identify bearing defects? If he didn't understand the customer implications? If he didn't have the confidence that his judgment would be respected?" Will nodded. "Exactly. Real empowerment isn't just giving people authority. It's building their capability to exercise that authority wisely and creating an environment where they feel safe to act on their judgment."

Over the next week, John began to see empowerment differently. It wasn't a program or an initiative. It wasn't something you announced and then checked off a list.

Empowerment was a fundamental reorientation of how power flowed through the organization.

He started paying attention to the moments when workers exercised real judgment and to the moments when they still deferred to authority even when they didn't need to.

In Cell 3, Rosa Washington had developed an informal quality check that caught defects the official inspection process missed. She'd been doing it for years, quietly, on her own time, because "nobody asked about it and I didn't want to get in trouble for doing something outside my job description."

John asked her to train others in her technique. She looked at him like he'd suggested she perform surgery. "Train them? But I'm not a trainer. I'm just a line worker."

"You're the person who knows more about catching these defects than anyone else in the building. That makes you the expert."

The training session Rosa eventually led was awkward at first, she wasn't used to being the authority in the room. But within an hour, her natural expertise took over, and John watched four other workers learn a technique that would prevent thousands of dollars in defects.

Afterward, Rosa found him in the hallway. "Twenty years," she said. "Twenty years I've been doing that check. Never told anyone because I figured they'd either ignore me or tell me to stop wasting time on things that weren't my job."

"What changed?"

She thought about it. "I guess I finally believe that someone actually wants to hear what I know."

That Sunday, John found himself at St. Brigid's, not for mass but for a conversation with Father Pat. The priest and his understanding of the plant's culture went deeper than most executives.

"You're wrestling with something," Father Pat said, pouring coffee in the rectory kitchen. "I can always tell."

"The CFO says we're manipulating workers. Using the language of empowerment to extract more labor without giving anything real in return."

Father Pat considered this. "And you're worried he might be right."

"I'm worried that the line between empowerment and exploitation is thinner than I thought. That I might cross it without realizing."

"Let me ask you something." Father Pat sat down across from him. "When Tommy told you the machine needed to move six inches, what did you do?"

"I moved it."

"You didn't calculate the ROI first? Didn't run it through a committee? Didn't ask for a written proposal with supporting documentation?"

"No. Will Moffitt told me to trust him."

"That's the difference." Father Pat leaned forward. "Exploitation asks: how can I get more from these people? Empowerment asks: how can I remove the obstacles that prevent these people from doing what they already know needs to be done? The CFO's world requires workers to prove their worth before being trusted. Your world, Will's world, starts with trust and builds from there."

"But what if they're wrong? What if their judgment is bad?"

"Then you coach them, develop them, help them understand what they missed. You don't take away their authority, you build their capability to use it better." Father Pat smiled. "That's what good teachers do. It's what good parents do. It's what good priests do, though we don't always succeed. Why should good managers be any different?"

The following Monday, John convened a special session for the workshop team, not to solve a problem, but to define what they were actually doing.

"I need your help understanding something," he told them. Tommy, Rosa, Bobby Santos, Maria, and a half-dozen others gathered around the scarred wooden table. "Some say empowerment is just a fancy word for getting workers to do management's thinking for free. I want to know what you think."

The silence stretched for an uncomfortable moment. Then Bobby Santos, the maintenance supervisor whose father had worked the line for forty years, spoke up.

"My dad had ideas. Hundreds of them. He'd come home and tell my mom about problems he'd seen, solutions he'd figured out. She'd ask why he didn't tell anyone at work, and he'd laugh. 'They don't pay me to think,' he'd say. 'They pay me to do what I'm told.'"

Bobby's voice tightened. "He died thinking his brain didn't matter. That's not empowerment, that's tragedy. What we are doing here is the opposite. It's finally letting people use what they've always had."

Rosa nodded. "The CFO thinks empowerment means giving something to workers. But we already have it, the knowledge, the ideas, the solutions. What you're giving us is permission to use it. And the support to use it well."

"And the trust to use it without fear," Tommy added. "That's the part most people miss. You can tell workers they're empowered all day long, but if they get punished for making a mistake, they'll stop taking risks. Real empowerment means accepting that people will sometimes be wrong, and that's okay. That's how learning happens."

John wrote on the whiteboard: Permission. Capability. Trust.

"Three legs of a stool," Will said from his seat in the corner. "Remove any one and it falls over. Tell people they're empowered but don't develop their capabilities, skills to solve, and you get chaos. Develop capabilities but don't give permission to act, and you get frustration. Give permission and capability but punish mistakes, and people stop taking risks."

"But there's something else," Maria said. "Something that matters more than any framework."

"What's that?"

"You have to be humble. Believe that the people doing the work are intelligent adults who want to do well. Believe that they have insights management will never have. Believe that treating them with respect isn't just good tactics, it's the right way to treat human beings." She paused. "Workers can tell the difference between a manager who sees them as assets to be optimized and one who sees them as people to be respected. Past management never understood that."

John looked around the table at the faces of people who had spent decades being ignored, who were now reshaping their own workplace. The numbers were impressive, eighteen percent productivity improvement, sixty percent reduction in defects, but they weren't what mattered.

What mattered was Tommy teaching a new hire the technique he'd developed over three decades, passing on knowledge that had finally been recognized as valuable. What mattered was Rosa standing in front of a room, confident for the first time at work that her expertise was worth sharing. What mattered was Stefan making a decision that prevented defective products from reaching customers and knowing his judgment would be respected rather than questioned.

Empowerment wasn't a management program. It wasn't a set of techniques or a framework or a way to extract more productivity from workers. It was a culture. It was recognition of something that had always been true: the people closest to the work understood it best, and any organization that ignored that understanding was operating at a fraction of its potential.

Six inches. Such a small distance. Such a long journey to understand what it really meant.

LESSONS LEARNED

The Three Kinds of Empowerment

Will Moffitt distinguishes between empowerment theater (announcements and posters that change nothing), delegation disguised as empowerment (authority to execute but not to think), and real empowerment (authority, capability, and support to make decisions about one's own work). Most organizations practice the first two while believing they've achieved the third. The test is simple: can workers change something about their work without asking permission, or must every improvement flow through layers of approval?

The Three Pillars: Permission, Capability, Trust

Real empowerment rests on three pillars. Permission means genuine authority to act, not just to suggest. Capability means the skills and knowledge to exercise good judgment. Trust means a safe environment where mistakes lead to learning rather than punishment. Remove any one pillar and empowerment collapses: permission without capability produces chaos; capability without permission produces frustration; both without trust produces paralysis.

Empowerment as Recognition, Not Gift

Workers already possess knowledge, intelligence, and problem-solving ability. Empowerment doesn't give them power, it removes the obstacles that prevent them from using the power they already have. As Rosa Washington observed, "What you're giving us is permission to use it." This reframing matters because it shifts the burden from workers proving their worth to management removing barriers.

The Authenticity Test

Workers can distinguish between managers who see them as assets to be optimized and those who see them as people to be respected. Empowerment implemented as a technique for better results never lasts. It must spring from genuine belief that people closest to the work understand it best. When John moved the machine six inches without calculating ROI or convening a committee, he demonstrated this belief in action. That's why the transformation took root where previous initiatives had failed.

Creating Value Connection

In *Creating Value*, Rizzo argues that sustainable improvement requires embedding problem-solving capability in the workforce itself. Top-down initiatives fade when consultants leave or leaders change. Empowerment is the mechanism by which this embedding occurs, not through training programs or quality circles, but through fundamentally changing how decisions are made and who makes them.

"Empowerment does not mean trying to figure out your job every day; that's chaos. Empowerment is being able to make changes to the standard of how the work is being done. Workers must follow the standard work every time. They do not get to deviate because we want consistent quality, productivity, customer experience, and safety. 'But wait a minute I have a better way.' Great, let's listen to the person doing the work and change the standard and that will be the way forward. The cumulative business impact of respect is enormous as you realize countless base hits by the people who do the work which add up to winning the game."

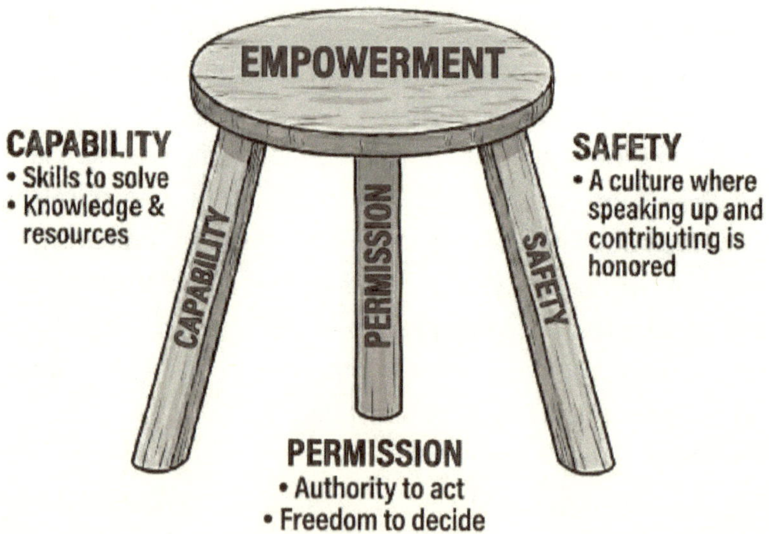

CHAPTER 7

The Resistance

"Defensive routines are anti-learning and overprotective."
— Chris Argyris

Not everyone celebrated the transformation. The COO, who had built his career on cost reduction through labor minimization, learned about the changes with growing alarm. Every worker empowered was, in his view, a worker who might demand higher wages. Every improvement implemented was proof that previous management had been inadequate. Every success was a threat to the worldview that had shaped his entire professional life.

His opposition took subtle forms at first, questions about methodology in executive meetings, requests for additional documentation, and suggestions that the improvements might not be sustainable. When these tactics failed to slow the momentum, he moved to direct interference.

"I've reviewed the productivity data," he had told the board at their quarterly meeting, his voice carrying the confidence of someone who believed numbers were objective truths rather than the choices people made about what to measure.

"The improvements are real, but they're coming at a cost. We're spending more on worker training, more on workshop facilitation, more on implementation support.
When you factor in the full cost, the ROI is marginal at best."

David Sterling had been prepared for this argument. John had anticipated the COO's resistance and provided detailed counter-analysis, showing that the "additional costs" cited were investments that would pay dividends for years to come, that the productivity improvements were accelerating rather than plateauing, and that worker engagement, measured through turnover rates and suggestion submissions, was at historically high levels.

But the COO had one card that facts couldn't counter: fear.

"What happens when these empowered workers start demanding more money? What happens when they realize they have leverage? We're building a monster that will eventually devour our profit margins."

The argument resonated with some board members, those who had been raised on the same management philosophy, who saw workers as costs to be minimized rather than assets to be developed. The discussion that followed revealed the deep divisions in American business thinking, the ongoing battle between those who believed in "power over" and those who were beginning to glimpse the potential of "power with".

In the end, the board voted to continue the program, but with increased oversight and quarterly reviews. It was a victory, but a conditional one, a recognition that the transformation remained vulnerable to those who saw workers as threats rather than partners.

The COO left the meeting with a thin smile that promised future resistance. The battle was far from over.

• • •

Fall 1993. The maples around Onondaga Lake had turned brilliant orange and red, as if nature itself was marking the transformation at Meridian with celebratory fire. But inside the plant, departed management had left a different kind of burn, the slow, systematic sabotage of everything John and the workers had built.

The first sign of organized resistance came on a Monday morning in September. John arrived to find his desk on the factory floor surrounded by yellow tape, a notice prominently displayed: "Violation of Administrative Safety Standards, Unauthorized Office Space in Production Area."

"Anonymous complaint," the inspector explained, clearly uncomfortable. "Someone reported that having a desk here violates six different safety regulations."

John knew who the anonymous someone was. But he also knew fighting it directly would play into their hands, making John look like he was putting his own preferences above worker safety.

"We'll comply immediately," John said, loud enough for the gathering workers to hear. "Safety comes first."

He moved his desk ten feet, just outside the technical production area but still visible from Line 3. Tommy Kowalski and several workers immediately moved their break benches closer, creating an informal office space that followed the letter of the regulation while violating its spirit entirely.

"Can't regulate where we take our breaks," Tommy said with a grin.

But the sabotage went deeper than petty harassment. Stefan Pomorski discovered it first, working late on the quarterly reports in his new role as CFO.

"John, you need to see this," Stefan said, calling him to the finance office. Spread across the desk were purchase orders, contracts, agreements, all dated in the last month, all bearing Morrison's signature from his time as CFO.

"He locked us into contracts," Stefan explained, his face pale in the fluorescent light. "Long-term purchase agreements at bad rates. Penalty clauses if we modify production schedules. Service contracts that prohibit us from doing our own maintenance. He's handcuffed us financially."

The numbers were staggering. Morrison had committed the company to expenses, all carefully structured to come due just as the transformation benefits should have shown on the bottom line.

"Can we void them?" John asked.

"Not without proving deliberate sabotage, which would require a legal battle we can't afford." Stefan rubbed his eyes, exhausted. "He's brilliant, in an evil way. Every contract is just barely defensible as prudent financial management."

The next morning, John called a meeting of the workshop leaders, Tommy, Rosa, Bobby Santos, Jennifer Chen, Father Pat. They needed to know what they were facing.

"They are trying to make us fail financially even while we succeed operationally," John explained. "We need to cut costs somewhere else to offset these contracts."

"Cut costs?" Rosa's voice was sharp with decades of suspicion. "That's always code for cutting people."

"Not this time," John said firmly. "We find savings without losing a single job. That's non-negotiable."

Bobby Santos looked at the contracts Stefan had spread out. "This maintenance agreement, it's with Morrison's brother-in-law's company. Charges us three times what our own mechanics cost."

"But we can't void it," Stefan said.

"No," Bobby agreed. "But look at the fine print. It only covers 'scheduled maintenance.' Everything else is extra. So we change our definition of scheduled versus unscheduled."

Jennifer was reading another contract. "This purchasing agreement specifies minimum order quantities but not the timing. We could pull and order when needed and not build inventory."

"Turn Morrison's weapons against him," Father Pat murmured. "There's something biblical about that."

They spent the day going through every contract, finding loopholes, workarounds, ways to minimize the damage. But it was exhausting, demoralizing work, energy that should have gone to improvement instead spent on defense.

The human cost became clear by week's end. Workers who had been energized by the transformation were now anxious, feeling the old familiar weight of management politics crushing their hopes. The suggestion box, now proudly unsealed and active, received fewer contributions. The workshops continued but with less enthusiasm.

"He's winning," Tommy said bitterly. "Not by stopping us directly but by making us tired."

It was Maria Santiago who recognized the deeper pattern. She appeared at John's makeshift office with a cardboard box full of union records.

"Morrison's not the first," she said. "This is what always happens. Look, 1978, after the strike. Management promised worker participation, then created so many rules and procedures that participation became meaningless. 1983, the

Quality Circle initiative. Killed by bureaucracy and infighting. 1987, the efficiency program. Sabotaged by middle managers who felt threatened."

She pulled out document after document, showing the pattern: hope, progress, resistance, failure.

"It's organizational scar tissue," she said. "Every time change threatens the power structure, antibodies form to fight it. This is just the current antibody."

Will Moffitt, who'd been listening, nodded slowly. "Chris Argyris wrote about this. Organizational defensive routines, the policies and actions that prevent embarrassment or threat but also prevent learning. They're not personal, they're systemic."

"So how do we fight back?" John asked.

"You don't fight it," Will said. "You expose it. You make the defensive routines visible, discussable. Sunlight and shadow, shadows can't survive in direct light."

That afternoon, John did something unprecedented. He called an all-hands meeting on the factory floor. All three shifts were invited, those off-duty came anyway, curious and concerned. Nearly four hundred workers gathered around the makeshift platform Bobby's team had constructed.

John laid out everything: the contracts, the financial constraints, the perceived threats to the power structure, the pattern of historical sabotage. He held nothing back, including his own frustration and fear.

"They want us to fail," he said. "Not because we're doing badly, but because we're doing well. Every improvement we make threatens people who benefit from the status quo. And they're fighting back with the only weapons they have, bureaucracy, contracts, administrative warfare."

The crowd was silent, processing this unusual honesty from management.

"So what do we do?" someone called out.

"We make it visible," John said. "Every obstacle, every piece of sabotage, every defensive routine. We document it, discuss it, overcome it together. They want to exhaust us with hidden battles. We're going to fight in the open."

Rosa Washington stood up. "I've got twenty years of documentation showing how good ideas get killed. Time to make it public."

Bobby Santos added, "Every maintenance problem Morrison's contracts create, we document. Show the board exactly what his agreements cost in downtime and quality."

One by one, workers stood, offering to document different aspects of the resistance they faced. It became a collective research project, mapping not just workflows but the organizational defenses that prevented improvement.

Jennifer Chen created an archive, scanning documents, and recording testimonies. Angela Kowalski interviewed older workers, capturing stories of past sabotage. Stefan tracked every financial impact of Morrison's contracts in real-time, creating a dashboard visible to anyone who wanted to see it.

The resistance from Morrison's allies intensified. Middle managers who'd been comfortable in the old system began creating obstacles. Change was seen as a failure of their leadership.

Paperwork requirements suddenly tripled. Meeting requests multiplied. Every improvement had to be justified with extensive documentation and ROI.

"Death by a thousand paper cuts," Tommy called it.

But something unexpected happened. The very act of documenting the resistance created solidarity among workers who'd previously been divided. First shift and second shift discovered they faced the same obstacles. Maintenance and production realized they had common antagonists. Even some middle managers, tired of being used as weapons against progress, began to defect to John's side.

The turning point came in October. Morrison had arranged for a surprise audit by an "independent" consulting firm, owned by his investment group. They arrived on a Monday morning with clipboards and authority, ready to find problems.

But the workers were ready. Every process was documented. Every improvement had data. Every suggestion implemented had clear attribution and results. The workers readily and accurately answered questions, backed by Angela's videos and Jennifer's databases.

The lead consultant, a sharp woman named Patricia Hayes, quickly realized what was happening. During a break, she pulled John aside.

"This isn't what we expected," she said quietly.

"What did you expect?"

"Chaos. Resentment. Evidence that worker empowerment leads to anarchy."

She looked at the floor, where Tommy was teaching a new employee the improved process, Rosa was updating quality charts, and Bobby's team was performing preventive maintenance.

"This is the opposite of chaos. Report that?"

Her report, delivered to the board two weeks later, was devastating to those who saw change as a failure of their leadership. She described a workforce more engaged than any she'd studied, improvements that rivaled best practices, and financial engineering that was clearly designed to make successful operations appear unsuccessful.

Morrison tried to discredit the report, claiming Patricia had been "compromised" by John's manipulation. But Elizabeth Hartwell had heard enough.

"Harold," she said during the board meeting John was invited to attend, "you've served this company for fifteen years. But I'm beginning to wonder who you've been serving."

"I've been serving shareholder value."

"You've been serving yourself," Hartwell interrupted. "These contracts you signed, your brother-in-law's maintenance firm, your golf partner's supply company, they're not arms-length transactions. They're conflict of interest at best, fraud at worst." Morrison's face went from red to white. "You can't prove…" "We don't need to prove anything in court," Hartwell said. "We just need to decide if you remain an advisor. All in favor of removing Harold Morrison from all positions with Meridian?" The vote was unanimous, even from board members Morrison had considered allies.

As Morrison was escorted out, he passed John in the hallway.

"You think you've won?" he hissed. "This plant will never sustain these changes. Workers always revert to laziness without proper supervision."

"You're wrong," John said calmly. "Workers don't revert to laziness. They revert to dignity. And dignity means wanting to do good work when given the chance."

Morrison left, but his contracts remained, legal obligations that would hamstring the company for two more years. John gathered the workshop leaders to figure out how to survive them.

"We can't void the contracts," Stefan said. "But we can offset them with improvements Morrison never imagined possible."

They launched what Tommy dubbed "Operation Jujitsu," using Morrison's constraints to create a sense of urgency and stimulate innovations. The expensive supply contracts motivated them to reduce material waste to unprecedented levels. The maintenance restrictions led to workers learning skills that made them more valuable and versatile.

"He tried to chain us," Rosa observed. "But chains can be broken if you're creative enough."

Father Pat offered theological perspective during a workshop break. "In the Bible, Joseph's brothers sold him into slavery, meaning evil. But God used it for good, saving all of Egypt from famine. Morrison meant these contracts for evil. We're using them for good."

The workers responded with ingenuity that surprised even John. Faced with supply constraints, they developed recycling processes that recovered materials previously scrapped. Blocked from routine maintenance, they invented preventive procedures that reduced breakdowns by eighty percent. Every obstacle became an opportunity for innovation.

By November, the transformation had survived its trial by fire. The workshops continued, now battle-tested. The suggestion program thrived, with workers confident their ideas would be implemented despite resistance. Most importantly, the culture had fundamentally shifted, from defensive to offensive, from accepting obstacles to overcoming them.

David Sterling addressed the plant. "What you've done here, exposing resistance, documenting sabotage, continuing to improve despite deliberate obstacles, this is more than operational excellence. This is organizational courage."

But it was old Eddie Zawicki who captured the real victory. During a workshop coffee break, he said, "You know what's different this time? When they tried to kill this transformation, we fought back. Together. That's never happened before. Management and workers on the same side, fighting the real enemy."

"Who's the real enemy?" Angela Kowalski asked, camera running.

"The belief that some people matter and some don't," Eddie said. "The lie that thinking and doing are separate. The system that says workers are costs, not assets. The enemy is the idea itself."

John thought of Anna Kowalski at Hawthorne, her brief moment of mattering. Of his grandfather, demoted for treating workers as humans. Of all the transformations that had failed not from bad ideas but from systematic resistance.

This time was different. Not because the ideas were better or the workers more capable, but because they'd made the resistance visible.

They'd named it, documented it, and overcome it together.

The workshops that resumed in late November had a different quality, harder earned, more precious, defended rather than granted. Workers knew they'd fought for the right to improve their own work and won.

"Transformation isn't a moment," Will Moffitt reflected, watching a cross-functional team redesign the shipping process. "It's a constant choice to resist reversion to old patterns. Today, we chose improvement."

The suggestion box, once sealed with tape, now stood open and full. The six-inch movement had become standard practice. The workshops continued their rhythm of improvement.

But most importantly, the workers had learned they could fight organizational defensive routines and win. They'd learned that resistance to change wasn't personal but systemic, and systems could be changed if enough people changed together.

Morrison's ghost still haunted the plant in the form of his contracts and the middle managers who'd been his allies. But ghosts have power only in darkness. And at Meridian, the lights were finally fully on.

The transformation had survived its first attempt at destruction.

Now it was time to prove it could thrive.

• • •

The crisis emerged without warning, as crises often do. A customer complaint revealed a pattern, a pattern that demanded explanation.

Three shipments in two weeks had been returned due to quality defects, the kind of obvious problems that should have been caught during inspection but somehow weren't.

"This is what happens when you let workers run things," some argued in an emergency meeting. "Discipline breaks down. Standards slip. The customer suffers."

But the investigation told a different story. The defects weren't caused by careless workers or slack supervision; they were caused by a systematic failure in the quality inspection process, specifically, by an "improvement" that management had implemented without consulting the workers who performed inspections.

Rosa Washington explained it with exasperation creeping into her voice. "Three months ago, someone in engineering decided that our inspection lights were not 'cost efficient' and needed to be replaced with 'approved' fixtures. The new lights are wrong; wrong color temperature, wrong angle, wrong intensity. We've been straining to see defects that the old lights would have made obvious.

"Why didn't anyone say something?" John asked.

Rosa's expression carried years of accumulated frustration. "We did say something. We filed complaints. We submitted suggestions. We talked to our supervisors. Nobody listened. The decision had been made, the new lights had been installed, and our concerns were dismissed as 'resistance to change'."

The investigation confirmed Rosa's account. Engineering records showed the light replacement had been approved based on cost savings alone, with no consultation from the workers who would be affected.

Inspection records showed a spike in defects beginning exactly when the new lights were installed. Worker feedback records showed multiple complaints that had not been acknowledged and ignored.

John presented the findings to the board. The better lights were restored within a week; the defect rate returned to normal within two.

But the more important outcome was systemic: a new policy requiring worker consultation before any change affecting work processes, and a formal review of all recent "improvements" that had been implemented without such consultation.

The quality crisis became a case study in exactly why the transformation was necessary, not because workers were perfect, but because workers knew things that managers didn't, and ignoring that knowledge had real costs.

LESSONS LEARNED

Organizational Antibodies

Sabotage represents a pattern that occurs whenever change threatens established power structures. The organization develops 'antibodies,' individuals and systems that fight to preserve the status quo. Understanding this pattern is essential for sustainable transformation: resistance is not personal but systemic, not accidental but predictable.

Argyris on Making the Undiscussable Discussable

Chris Argyris taught that organizational change requires surfacing defensive routines, making visible the hidden patterns that prevent learning. John's decision to share Morrison's sabotage publicly follows Argyris's prescription: sunlight and shadow, shadows can't survive in direct light.

Creating Value Connection

In *Creating Value*, Rizzo acknowledges that transformation is always contested. Those who benefit from current arrangements and lack humility will resist changes that threaten their position. Sustainable change requires not just implementing improvements but building teams strong enough to sustain improvements.

CHAPTER 8

The Wisdom of Generations

"Experience by itself teaches nothing. Without theory, experience has no meaning. Without theory, one has no questions to ask. Hence, without theory, there is no learning."

— *W. Edwards Deming*

Winter 1993-1994. The lake-effect snow that year was relentless, blanketing Syracuse in white from Thanksgiving through March. But inside Meridian, something warm was happening, the systematic excavation of buried wisdom, decades of worker knowledge finally being brought into the light.

It started with a literal excavation. The old administrative building, damaged by frozen pipes during the Christmas shutdown, needed renovation. When the construction crew broke through a wall to assess the damage, they found a storage room.

John got the call at 5 AM from Pete Wojcik, the night janitor who'd discovered it. "Mr. Valerio, you need to see this. Bring a flashlight."

The room was a tomb of ambition then neglect. Floor to ceiling filing cabinets, every drawer labeled by year and department: production reports, drawings for tooling and parts long ago retired, project folders, capital requests, and additional suggestions thought lost.

And on a desk in the corner, covered in dust, a coffee mug with the words "Suggestion Program" and a calendar still showing October 1987.

"Jesus Christ," Tommy Kowalski whispered, having arrived with the first shift. He pulled open a drawer at random, 1962, Line 3. Inside were hundreds of suggestions, each on a standard form, each carefully typed or handwritten.

"These are all..."

"Worker suggestions," Will Moffitt finished, leaning heavily on his cane. The climb to the sealed room had winded him, but his eyes were sharp with recognition. "Every single one submitted over the years."

John picked up a suggestion at random, dated March 1943. Rose Santos, Bobby's grandmother, proposing quality checks at the source rather than at the end of production. The idea that had taken them nine months to "discover" in 1993.

The patterns that emerged were heartbreaking and inspiring in equal measure.

1927: Stefan Kowalski, Tommy's great-grandfather, suggested reorganizing workflow to reduce motion waste. Never implemented. The same suggestion appeared from different workers over the years. Forty years of workers seeing the same problem, proposing the same solution, being ignored with identical consistency.

"We implemented this in January," Tommy said quietly. "Productivity went up twenty percent. Forty years it could have been better."

1952: Tony Valerio proposed the six-inch machine movement. But he wasn't alone, seventeen different workers over thirty years had suggested similar adjustments to their specific equipment. Small movements that would have accumulated into transformation.

"Death by a thousand ignored improvements," Father Pat said during one review session. "Each rejection not just of an idea but of a person's dignity."

The finance suggestions were particularly painful. Workers had identified cost savings that may have prevented three layoff cycles.

As word spread about the discovery, older workers and retirees began visiting, looking for their suggestions, their fathers' suggestions, evidence that their intelligence had at least been documented if not valued.

Salvatore Benedetti, eighty-three, found his 1959 proposal for cross-training workers. "I said workers should learn multiple jobs, help each other, cover for illness without losing production. They said it would 'confuse responsibilities.' Now Toyota does exactly this and we study them like geniuses."

The most poignant discovery came from Maria Santiago. In a box labeled "1978-1979 Strike Resolution," she found her father Miguel's notebook. Not an official suggestion but a personal journal he'd submitted desperately, hoping someone would read it.

"I write this in English though it is not my first language because I want management to understand. We do not strike from greed. We strike from grief. Every day we see waste, wasted material, wasted time, wasted intelligence. We know how to fix these problems. Our hands have solutions our mouths are not permitted to speak. Please, I beg, let us help make this company better. Let us use our minds as well as our backs."

Maria sighed, holding the journal. "He died thinking no one ever read this."

"We're reading it now," John said. "And we're going to act on it."

They created what Jennifer called the Archive of Lost Intelligence, a digital repository of every idea, searchable, creditable, analyzable. But more than that, they created a memorial to ignored wisdom.

In the main hallway, where every worker would pass, they installed a display: "The Wall of Wisdom." Each day featured a different historical suggestion with the submitter's name, their idea, and when possible, a photograph. Below each, a placard showed what implementing the suggestion would have saved or improved.

January 15, 1994: Rose Santos (1943) - Quality at Source Could have prevented untold defects. January 16, 1994: Tony Valerio (1952) - Six-Inch Machine Adjustment Would have saved thousands of hours of wasted motion. January 17, 1994: Miguel Santiago (1971) - Cross-Training Program Could have prevented the 1981 layoffs entirely. The wall became a pilgrimage site. Workers would stop, read, sometimes recognize a name; a father, grandfather, neighbor long dead. The accumulated weight of ignored intelligence was staggering, undeniable.

Another strong response came from an unexpected source. A delegation from Japan stood transfixed before the Wall.

"This is remarkable," their lead engineer, Takeshi Yamamoto, said.

"These suggestions from the 1940s and 1950s, they're similar to what we implemented in the 1960s and 1970s.

Your workers could have invented a business system before we did. They just weren't allowed to implement it."

He pointed to specific suggestions: Tony Valerio's quick changeover methods, Rose Santos's quality at source, Miguel Santiago's cross-training, all pillars of what the world now studied as Japanese innovation.

"We learned from American workers when we visited in the 1950s," Mr. Yamamoto continued. "But we learned from workers, not management. We listened to people like these" he gestured at the wall, "because in Japan, we had no choice. We had no resources except human intelligence. You had resources, so you could afford to waste intelligence."

David Sterling arranged for Mr. Yamamoto to address the entire plant. The Japanese engineer stood before four hundred workers and delivered a message none of them expected: "Meridian workers, we owe you a debt. Your ideas, ignored here, inspired our transformation. We succeeded with your wisdom. Now you must reclaim what was always yours."

The impact was electric. Workers who'd internalized decades of being told they were the problem suddenly understood they'd always been the solution.

The Japanese delegation, preparing to leave, made one final observation.

Mr. Yamamoto pulled John aside.

"You know what's different here from most American factories trying to implement continuous improvement?" he asked.

"What?" "You're not copying Toyota. You're reclaiming Meridian. You're building your own business system.

Finding your own way. You're becoming what you always should have been. That's why it will last."

• • •

The workshops that followed took on a different character, not only of innovation but reclamation. They became celebrations of collective wisdom rather than struggles against institutional ignorance. Ideas flowed freely. They would find a current problem, then not only listen to those doing the work, but listen to those in the past. Almost always, someone had thought of the improvement years or decades earlier.

"We're not inventing," Rosa Washington said during one workshop. "We're remembering."

The maintenance team discovered that Bobby Santos's father had designed a productive maintenance system in 1968 that anticipated modern computer-aided approaches. Bobby found the lists of tasks for operators and maintenance workers.

They implemented his father's system, adapting it with modern tools but keeping the core logic. Equipment failures dropped in two months.

The archives revealed another pattern, families of intelligence. The Kowalskis: four generations of workflow improvements. The Santos family: three generations of maintenance innovations. The Valerio-Santiago connection: Tony and Miguel had collaborated on dozens of suggestions, an Italian-Mexican partnership that management never knew existed.

"Intelligence runs in families," Father Pat observed. "Not genetic but cultural. Parents teaching children to observe, to think, to solve. Even when no one listened, they kept teaching."

Angela Kowalski was documenting everything, creating a film that would eventually be titled "Ghosts in the Machine: A Century of Silenced Wisdom." She interviewed children and grandchildren of suggestion-makers, capturing stories that had been preserved in family lore.

"My grandmother Rose," Bobby said to Angela's camera, "she'd come home from work and redesign our kitchen based on motion efficiency. Said if Meridian wouldn't use her ideas, at least her family would benefit. Our kitchen was the most efficient in Syracuse. Still is."

The film captured something else, the healing happening as ignored intelligence was finally acknowledged. Workers walked taller.

But the most profound discovery came in February 1994. In a box mislabeled "Miscellaneous 1920s," Jennifer found something extraordinary, a correspondence between Meridian workers and Mary Parker Follett herself.

The letters, dated 1928-1929, showed that Follett had visited Syracuse, met with workers, and tried to convince management to implement what she called "integration of worker intelligence."

One letter, from a worker named Giovanni Torretti, Joey's great-grandfather, described Follett's visit: "She came to the floor, this lady professor from Boston. But she didn't watch us like the time-study men. She asked us questions. Real questions. What did we think? How would we improve? She wrote everything down, said she would include our ideas in her book. Management threw her out after two days. Said she was 'disrupting productivity.' But for two days, we mattered."

John read the letter aloud at an all-hands meeting. The plant fell silent, processing this connection between their current transformation and a visitor from sixty-five years ago.

"Mary Parker Follett was here," John said. "She saw what you had to offer. She tried to make management listen. We're sixty-five years late, but we're finally finishing what she started."

Will Moffitt, who'd been Follett's intellectual disciple his entire career, stood with tears in his eyes. "She would be so proud. Not of management finally listening, but of workers finally being heard."

The discoveries kept coming. A complete training system designed by women workers during World War II, ignored when the men returned.

Safety improvements proposed by injured workers, dismissed as complaints rather than solutions. Cost-saving measures suggested during every recession, implemented only after layoffs had decimated the workforce.

Stefan created a financial analysis of the accumulated impact. If Meridian had implemented just fifty percent of worker suggestions over the past, the company would be worth multiple times its current value.

"We didn't just ignore suggestions," Stefan reported to the board. "We ignored people.

A recognition ceremony took place in March, exactly one year after the six-inch move. The plant floor was transformed into an auditorium. Workers, retirees, families filled every space.

Tommy Kowalski accepted for his great-grandfather Stefan. Bobby Santos for his grandmother Rose. Maria Santiago for her father Miguel.

When Tony Valerio's name was called, John stood, along with forty other workers.

"Tony helped all of us with suggestions," explained Eddie Zawicki.

"Even when his own were ignored, he kept helping others write theirs. He never gave up believing that someday, someone would listen."

The ceremony lasted three hours. Many suggestions formally acknowledged, their owners named, their impact estimated. The accumulated wisdom of generations finally brought into the light.

But the real transformation was in what happened next. The suggestion rate exploded, daily improvements accelerated, not because of the bonuses but because of the belief.

Workers who'd held back ideas for years suddenly shared freely. The archive became not just history but inspiration, proof that workers had always known how to improve their work.

"We're not teaching them anything new," Will Moffitt reflected, watching a workshop where three generations collaborated on solving a problem. "We're just finally admitting they never needed teaching. They needed permission. They needed respect. They needed someone to say their intelligence mattered."

As winter turned to spring, the Archive of Lost Intelligence continued growing, not with old suggestions but with new ones, building on the foundation of the old. Workers would reference historical proposals, improve them with modern knowledge, create synthesis across generations.

The Wall of Wisdom grew like a tree. Every improvement got added, with full attribution, creating a living history of recognized intelligence.

Tommy Kowalski, standing before his great-grandfather's suggestion finally implemented after sixty-seven years, summed up the transformation: "They thought they were burying our ideas. Turns out they were planting seeds. Just took a while for spring to come."

Spring had come to Meridian. And with it, the flowering of intelligence that had been waiting in the dark, preserved in filing cabinets and family stories, ready to bloom when someone finally provided the light of recognition.

The transformation wasn't new. It had been proposed, documented, and ignored for seventy years.

Now, finally, it was being implemented.

Six inch moves at a time. One suggestion at a time. One recognized intelligence at a time.

The wisdom of generations, unearthed and unleashed at last.

LESSONS LEARNED

The Archive as Organizational Memory

The room containing years of worker suggestions represents accumulated wisdom systematically ignored.

Each suggestion was a moment when a worker cared enough to propose an improvement, believed enough to commit it to paper, and hoped enough to submit it through official channels.

Intergenerational Knowledge Transfer

Tommy discovering his grandfather's 1952 suggestion, essentially identical to his own recent proposal, illustrates how organizational knowledge can persist across generations even when formally suppressed. Families pass down not just stories but insights, not just grievances but solutions.

Creating Value Connection

Creating Value emphasizes that every organization possesses latent capabilities waiting to be activated. The task of leadership is to create conditions where this knowledge can surface, where historical wisdom can inform current practice.

PART THREE: REDEMPTION
1994-1995

CHAPTER 9

The Transformation Accelerates

"The Toyota style is not to create results by working hard. It is a system that says there is no limit to people's creativity. People don't go to Toyota to 'work'—they go there to 'think.'"

— Taiichi Ohno

Spring 1994. The resilient crocuses in the garden pushed through the cold ground, purple and yellow vibrant against the lingering, dingy crust of snow

Inside Meridian, a similar renewal was occurring, not just of ideas but of human ingenuity.

News of Meridian's transformation spread beyond Syracuse, carried by industry publications, academic papers, and the informal networks that connected manufacturing professionals across the country.

John stood in what had once been the executive conference room, now transformed into Mission Control for the plant-wide transformation. The mahogany table Morrison had imported from Italy had been replaced with plywood on sawhorses, covered in layouts, schedules, and tracking charts. Twenty-five workshops were scheduled for the year; they'd already completed seventeen, and it was only April.

"We have a problem," David Sterling announced, entering with uncharacteristic energy. "A good problem, but a problem."

The core team gathered, Tommy, Rosa, Bobby, Jennifer, Stefan, Father Pat, and Will Moffitt, who moved slower each day but insisted on being present for every major decision.

"Three local companies want to visit," Sterling continued. "General Motors, Carrier, and Lockheed Martin. They've heard about our transformation and want to learn how we did it."

The week before their arrival, something unexpected happened. The night shift who produced enclosures, traditionally the most resistant to change, had requested their own workshop.

"We've been watching," their representative, Andre Williams, told John. "Watching Line 3, watching day shift, watching everyone else get better while we stayed the same. We're tired of being the weak link." Their workshop focus was radical, complete elimination of the shift itself, not through layoffs but through redistribution. They proposed becoming a floating team, filling gaps across all shifts, becoming the plant's rapid response unit for problems and opportunities.

They were available to do this because they had already made improvements in their area that freed up twenty-two workers. Management was shocked and asked why they were not told about this capacity. The response: "We never trusted you as partners before."

"We know every job," Andre explained. "Night shift always does. We have to cover for everyone with skeleton crews. Make that our strength instead of our burden." The workshop revealed something profound. Night shift hadn't been resistant to change, they'd been invisible to it. Every improvement had been designed for day shift rhythms, day shift supervision, day shift social dynamics.

"We're ghosts," one night worker said. "We come in when you leave, fix what broke during the day, keep the place running, then disappear before you return. Nobody knows our names, our ideas, our capabilities."

Jennifer Chen started documenting night shift innovations, discoveries that amazed even veteran day workers. The night crew had developed a complete shadow system of improvements, unofficial but effective, implemented without permission because no one was watching.

"This is brilliant," Stefan said, reviewing their self-designed system. "You've been running a parallel factory, optimized for different constraints."

"We had to," Andre said. "Management sleeps at night. We had to manage ourselves."

The transformation of night shift into the Rapid Response Team became a model for autonomous work groups. They kept their shift differential but gained something more valuable, visibility, recognition, and the official mandate to solve problems wherever they emerged.

When a delegation from a local company arrived, twelve executives and engineers were met not by Sterling or John but by Andre Williams, Tommy Kowalski and Rosa Washington.

"Welcome to Meridian," Tommy said. "We're going to show you something different. Not how management transformed a factory, but how workers transformed themselves when management finally got out of the way."

The tour began at the Wall of Wisdom. Rosa explained the history of ignored intelligence, the recent excavation of buried suggestions, the implementation of ideas that had waited decades for respect.

"You mean," one executive said slowly, "workers had already proposed most of your improvements?"

"Our grandparents proposed them," Tommy corrected. "We're just finally implementing them."

They moved to Line 3, where Rosa Martinez demonstrated the difference between the old and new methods. She showed them the six-inch movement, explaining how such a small change cascaded into transformation.

"But surely," an engineer protested, "management must have directed this, coordinated it, controlled it?" "Management listened," Rosa said simply. "That's all. We did the rest."

The delegation grew increasingly uncomfortable as the tour continued. They'd expected to learn about management techniques, leadership strategies, organizational structures. Instead, they were learning about trust, respect, and the intelligence that had always existed on their own factory floors.

Bobby Santos showed them the maintenance system, explaining how his father's design had been more sophisticated than current computer systems. "The solution was always here. It was just buried under disrespect."

Angela Kowalski presented footage from workshops, showing workers teaching engineers, hourly teaching salary, old teaching young, young teaching old, knowledge flowing in all directions without regard for hierarchy.

"This is chaos," one executive muttered.

"No," Father Pat corrected gently. "This is empowerment. Order arising from culture, not imposed from above."

The most powerful moment came during lunch. Instead of eating in the executive dining room, the delegation ate in the regular cafeteria with workers. They sat at long tables, sharing stories, and slowly, carefully, the workers among the delegation began to speak.

"We have ideas too," one said quietly. "For years no one's ever asked my opinion about my own job."

"They ask," another worker corrected. "They just don't hear. There's a difference."

By afternoon, the tour had become something else, a therapy session for their own frustrated workforce. Their workers were pulling John and Tommy aside, asking how to start workshops, how to get management to listen, and how to prove their intelligence mattered.

"You can't make them listen," Tommy said. "But you can make ignoring you expensive. Make waste visible."

The executives left shaken. Their feedback, delivered to Sterling a week later, was telling: "The Meridian transformation is not replicable through traditional means. It requires a fundamental shift in power dynamics that most organizations are not prepared to make."

But word spread anyway. Not through executive networks but through worker networks. UAW Syracuse members talked to Steelworkers who talked to Teamsters. The story of Meridian became labor folklore, the plant where workers won not through strikes but through harnessing intelligence. One union official's message was clear: "I can't negotiate with a company that is failing. I can with one that respects workers and is succeeding."

More workshops launched, now worker-initiated rather than management-scheduled. The packaging department redesigned their entire workflow in a weekend. The shipping team eliminated two days from delivery cycles. The receiving department created a quality inspection system that caught vendor problems before they entered production.

Each workshop followed the same pattern that Will Moffitt had learned from Follett and McGregor, circular response, power-with, integration rather than domination. Ideas built on ideas, creating solutions no individual could have imagined.

"It's like jazz," Father Pat observed during one particularly creative session. "Everyone playing their own instrument, but listening to each other, creating something that emerges from the collective."

The twenty-five workshop goal was exceeded by June. But more importantly, workshops were no longer events, they were continuous. Mini-workshops happened during breaks, informal improvement sessions during lunch, problem-solving that didn't wait for official sanction. Daily improvement.

Stefan tracked the macro impact obsessively, partly to prove the value, partly because he couldn't believe the numbers. He did not try to calculate an ROI for every single improvement. That would be like trying to determine which specific workout made an athlete faster.

"We continue to improve quality, delivery, and cost. We're steadily gaining market share," he reported to the board in July. "Not through cost-cutting but through intelligence-unleashing. Every worker is essentially a consultant better than any we could hire."

Elizabeth Hartwell pushed for more aggressive transformation. "If this works at Meridian, it could work at our other plants."

"No," John said firmly, surprising everyone. "You can adopt the system but can't copy the improvements. Each plant must find its own way, its own buried intelligence, its own six-inch movements. We can share the principle but not the prescription."

Will Moffitt, increasingly frail but still sharp, added historical context. "This is what Follett understood that Taylor didn't. You can't standardize human creativity. Each organization has to grow its own."

The summer brought unexpected challenges. The success at Meridian had attracted union attention, not from local unions, who were thrilled, but from national leadership worried about precedent.

"You're breaking down the barriers between management and labor," a national UAW representative told Maria Santiago. "That's dangerous."

"Dangerous to who?" Maria shot back. "To workers who are finally being heard? Or to union leaders who built careers on conflict?"

The conversation revealed a deeper issue. The transformation threatened not just management hierarchies but union hierarchies, consultant industries, and the entire ecosystem that profited from labor-management conflict.

"We're proving the conflict is artificial," Tommy told John after a tense meeting with union nationals. "That threatens everyone who benefits from the war."

But the workers weren't interested in maintaining artificial conflicts. They were too busy improving their work, their workplace, their lives. Every employee was implementing at least one improvement every week.

"In the old days," Rosa reflected, "suggestions were where ideas went to die. Now they're where ideas go to multiply."

The multiplication was literal. Workers would build on each other's suggestions, creating improvement chains. Joey Torretti suggested a tool reorganization. Bobby Santos improved it with color coding. Rosa Martinez added shadow boards. Andre Williams created a checkout system.

Four suggestions becoming one integrated solution.

The Rapid Response Team, formerly night shift, had become the plant's innovation engine. Free to move between departments, shifts, and problems, they cross-pollinated solutions, carrying improvements like bees carrying pollen.

"We're not managing anymore," Sterling told the board. "We're gardening. Creating conditions for growth rather than controlling the growth itself."

Some board members were uncomfortable with this loss of traditional control. But Hartwell silenced doubters with simple math: "Meridian is now our most profitable plant. Whatever they're doing, we should interfere as little as possible."

The workshops evolved into teaching opportunities. Experienced workers became trainers, not of tasks but of thinking. They taught observation, waste identification, root cause analysis, solution generation, metacognitive skills that traditional training ignored.

Old Eddie Zawicki, who'd initially been skeptical, became one of the most effective teachers. "I'm not teaching them my job," he explained. "I'm teaching them how I learn. There's a difference."

The difference was generative rather than replicative learning. Workers weren't copying solutions but learning to create solutions. The plant was developing what Chris Argyris called "double-loop learning": not just fixing problems within existing assumptions, but questioning the assumptions themselves, and it was happening from the bottom up rather than from the top down.

In August, something unprecedented happened. A customer, Westhouse, asked to meet not with sales or management but with the workers who made their components.

"We want to understand your quality improvements," the Westhouse engineer explained. "Our receiving inspection shows zero defects for six weeks. That's impossible."

Rosa Washington led the customer meeting, explaining her quality at the source system, now enhanced by twenty workers' contributions. She showed them how defects were prevented rather than detected, how quality was built in rather than inspected in.

"This is more sophisticated than our own quality system," the Westhouse engineer admitted. "Would you consider consulting for us?" The room went silent. Rosa Washington, a Black woman who'd been denied promotion for twenty years was being asked to consult for a Fortune 500 company.

"I'll consider it," she said with confidence that filled the room. "But I won't leave Meridian. This is where my knowledge was born. This is where it belongs."

The request sparked a new possibility. Workers as consultants to customers, suppliers, even competitors. Not selling products but selling intelligence, knowledge, and wisdom.

"We're not a manufacturing company anymore," Jennifer observed. "We're a learning company that happens to manufacture."

By September, when the leaves turned gold and orange around the lake, the transformation was complete enough to be self-sustaining. New workers were onboarded not by HR but by experienced workers. Problems were solved by those closest to them. Improvements emerged continuously without management intervention.

Will Moffitt, watching from his chair in the War Room because he could no longer stand for long periods, saw his life's work fulfilled. "Mary Parker Follett wrote about this in 1924," he said. "Power-with creating expanding circles of capability. It only took seventy years to prove her right."

The workshops had achieved their goal, not just the twenty-five planned but forty-three completed, with dozens more informal sessions. But more importantly, they'd changed the fundamental dynamic of the plant.

"We don't work for Meridian anymore," Tommy said during a celebration of the year's achievements. "We are Meridian. The company isn't the buildings or machines or even the products. It's us, our knowledge, our improvements, our collective intelligence."

Father Pat offered a benediction at the celebration: "In the beginning was the word, and the word was 'No', no to suggestions, no to intelligence, no to dignity. Now the word is 'Yes', yes to ideas, yes to improvements, yes to the fundamental truth that every human being has something to contribute."

The transformation had accelerated beyond anyone's imagination. But velocity wasn't the real achievement. The real achievement was direction, not top-down but omni-directional, improvement flowing from every person to every other person, creating a web of intelligence that no competitor could replicate.

Standing among hundreds of workers at the celebration, John thought of his grandfather, demoted for believing in worker intelligence. Tony would have loved this, not the success but the recognition, the dignity, and the simple acknowledgment that the people doing the work already knew how to do it better.

"We're not done," Rosa Washington said, standing beside him. "This is just the beginning. We've proven workers can transform a plant. Now we prove we can sustain it, grow it, make it the new normal."

She was right. The transformation had accelerated, but acceleration wasn't the end, it was the means. The end was a workplace where every intelligence mattered, every voice was heard, every six-inch improvement was valued.

They'd achieved power-with instead of power-over.

Now they had to keep it.

LESSONS LEARNED

From Events to Culture

The transformation accelerated when workshops stopped being special events and became normal practice. This shift from program to culture marks the difference between temporary improvement and sustainable transformation.

Japanese Auto Industry and the American Rediscovery

The Japanese delegation's recognition of Meridian's methods as kindred to their own represents a historical irony. Their production system drew heavily on principles American thinkers like Follett, Mayo, McGregor and Deming had articulated decades earlier. The Japanese system was American wisdom, refined abroad and returned home.

Creating Value Connection

In *Creating Value*, Rizzo describes the characteristics of self-sustaining improvement systems: clear principles widely understood, distributed decision-making authority, visible feedback on results, and consistent recognition of contributions.

CHAPTER 10

The Boardroom Battle

"Management cannot provide a man with self-respect or with the respect of his fellows or with the satisfaction of needs for self-fulfillment. It can create conditions such that he is encouraged and enabled to seek such satisfactions for himself, or it can thwart him by failing to create those conditions."

— *Douglas McGregor*

July 4th Weekend. Independence Day, a fitting date for what would become Meridian's declaration of independence from the tyranny of value extraction. Harold Morrison had chosen the holiday weekend carefully, assuming workers would be dispersed, management would be vacationing, and his corporate raid could proceed unopposed.

He was wrong.

The news had leaked Thursday evening. Jennifer Chen, monitoring company emails as part of her new role in information systems, spotted the board meeting notice buried in technical amendments. Emergency session, July 4th, 2 PM. Single agenda item: "Strategic Alternatives for Shareholder Value Maximization."

"That's corporate speak for selling us off," Stefan translated, his face pale in the computer screen's glow.

John immediately called Tommy, Rosa, Bobby, Father Pat, and the other workshop leaders. By midnight Thursday, phone trees, the old-fashioned kind, person calling person, had activated throughout Syracuse. Workers who hadn't spoken in years were suddenly coordinating.

"My father fought in World War II," Eddie Zawicki said at the impromptu gathering in the union hall. "He didn't fight so some Wall Street vulture could destroy American jobs for profit. I'll be there Saturday if I have to crawl."

By Friday afternoon, despite the holiday, the plant parking lot was full. Workers weren't working, production was shut down for the long weekend, but they were preparing. Jennifer coordinating information, Angela documenting everything, and Stefan running financial scenarios.

"Morrison's brought in Blackpave Capital," Stefan reported, pulling up SEC filings. "Richard Blackpave himself is flying in. They're offering $150 million for the company, about sixty percent of real value, but the board might take it because it's immediate cash."

"What happens to us if they buy?" Rosa Martinez asked.

"Standard Blackpave playbook," Stefan said grimly. "Keep the customers and patents, sell the real estate, offshore production. Maybe keep some jobs here for appearances. Everyone else gone within eighteen months."

The room erupted in angry voices, but Tommy's cut through: "Then we stop them."

"How?" someone asked. "We're workers, not board members."

"We're more than workers," Rosa Washington said, standing with quiet authority. "We're the company. Without us, they're buying empty buildings and silent machines."

Father Pat had been quietly working his networks, both religious and community. By Friday evening, he reported remarkable news: "The Syracuse pension fund is interested. The teachers' union. Several local investors who remember when Meridian mattered to this city. If we can match Blackpave's offer..."

They worked through Friday night, assembling not a counter-offer but a counter-narrative. Every improvement documented. Every cost saving calculated. Every future innovation projected. The Wall of Remembered Wisdom photographed and cataloged. The workshop results were bound and tabulated.

"This isn't just numbers," Will Moffitt said, overseeing the preparation despite exhaustion. "This is evidence that value creation beats value extraction every time, if given the chance."

Saturday morning dawned hot and humid, unusual for Syracuse. By noon, over two thousand people had gathered outside corporate headquarters, not just workers but families, children, retirees, community members. They weren't protesting in the traditional sense.

Instead, they were demonstrating.

Bobby Santos and his maintenance team had assembled a working production line in the parking lot, showing improvements in real-time. Rosa and Michael demonstrated the new methods versus old, letting anyone try both.

Rosa Washington ran quality demonstrations, teaching children to spot defects, proving that anyone could learn if properly taught.

"We're not asking for charity," Tommy announced through a bullhorn.

"We're showing value. Real value, not financial engineering." Inside the boardroom, Harold Morrison was making his pitch to twelve board members. Richard Blackpave sat beside him, silver-haired, sharp-suited, radiating the confidence of someone who'd bought and monetized dozens of companies.

"The numbers are clear," Morrison said, his PowerPoints full of decline narratives. "Labor costs too high. Productivity is too low. Market share eroding. Blackpave's offer provides shareholders with immediate liquidity and certain value."

"Certain value through destruction," David Sterling countered. "Mr. Morrison, you spent five years sabotaging this company to make it look weak. Your contracts alone cost us two million in unnecessary expenses."

"Ancient history," Blackpave interrupted smoothly. "What matters is the future. And the future of manufacturing is not in Syracuse. It's in Mexico, China, wherever labor is cheapest."

"Unless labor is also smart," John said from the doorway.

He'd arrived with his team, Tommy, Rosa, Stefan, Jennifer, and surprisingly, Will Moffitt, who'd insisted on attending despite his fatigue.

"This is a closed session," Morrison protested.

"No," Elizabeth Hartwell said firmly. "If we're deciding the fate of four hundred workers, they should be represented. Continue, Mr. Valerio."

John didn't use PowerPoints. Instead, he and his team brought products, actual components manufactured using the old methods and new, letting board members feel the quality difference, see the improvements.

Tommy spoke first, not from notes but from his heart: "For most of those years, I've been told that my job is to do what I'm told, follow the procedures, keep my ideas to myself. And for most of those years, I did exactly that, because what choice did I have? This year has been different. For the first time in my life, someone asked me what I thought. Someone listened when I answered. Someone acted on what I said. Someone was teaching us how to solve problems and make improvements. And you know what happened? I started caring again. Started thinking again. Started believing that my work actually mattered. That's what you're really deciding today. Not just whether to accept some buyout offer, but whether workers like me have any value beyond our hands. Whether our wisdom matters. Whether this company is going to be a place where people come to contribute or just a place where people come to collect a paycheck until they can escape."

"You can move machines to China," Stefan said. "You can't move generations of knowledge, relationships, improvements. Those die when the plant closes. And once dead, they can't be resurrected."

Blackpave laughed, a sound like ice cracking. "Touching stories, but business isn't about sentiment. It's about returns. I'm offering guaranteed returns today."

"And we're offering something better," a new voice said from the doorway. Maria Santiago entered, followed by representatives from unions, pension funds, and community organizations. Behind her, visible through the boardroom windows, the parking lot demonstration continued, workers showing their value in real-time.

"We've assembled a counter-offer," Maria announced. "An Employee Stock Ownership Plan (ESOP) backed by local investors, pension funds, and workers themselves. Not to buy the company but to invest in it. To become partners in value creation rather than victims of value extraction."

"Ha, it's less than Blackpave," Morrison said dismissively.

Elizabeth Hartwell said slowly. "Mr. Blackpave, what's your five-year projection for Meridian?"

Blackpave shrugged. "Meridian probably won't exist in five years. The assets will be redistributed to more profitable ventures."

"Mr. Valerio, your five-year projection?" John looked at his team, at Will Moffitt, who nodded encouragement despite his pain, at the workers visible through the windows. "In five years, Meridian will be the model for American manufacturing renaissance. Every improvement we've made will compound. Every worker we've empowered will empower others. We'll be worth not 150 million but 5 times that and still growing."

"Fantasy," Morrison spat.

"Is it?" Hartwell asked. "Mr. Santos, would you come in please?"

Bobby Santos entered, uncomfortable in the boardroom but determined. "Blackpave offers to buy our past and destroy our future," Bobby said. "These workers offer to invest in a future we'll build together. Which creates more value?"

The boardroom fell silent. Through the windows, the demonstration continued, children learning quality inspection from Rosa Washington, retirees teaching young workers forgotten techniques, the entire community engaged in showing what Meridian could be.

"I need to share something," board member Samuel Morrison said suddenly. All eyes turned to Harold Morrison's father, elderly, quiet, who'd barely spoken in years of board meetings.

"I've been on this board for thirty years," the elder Morrison said.

"I've watched my son systematically destroy this company to make it buyable. I stayed quiet out of paternal loyalty. But loyalty to what? To manipulation? To destruction? To the waste of human potential?"

He stood, shaky but determined. "My father worked at Meridian. Assembly line, 1932 to 1967. He had ideas, innovations, improvements. All ignored. He died believing he was just a pair of hands. I became successful, got rich, joined boards, but I never forgot his bitterness. And now my son wants to create four hundred more bitter workers, four hundred more wasted potentials."

He looked directly at Harold. "I failed as a father if this is what I taught you. But I won't fail as a board member." He turned to the room. "I move to reject Blackpave's offer and accept the worker investment proposal."

"Seconded," Elizabeth Hartwell said immediately.

"This is insane," Blackpave protested. "You're choosing sentiment over certainty."

"No," Hartwell replied. "We're choosing value creation over value extraction. We're choosing sustainable growth over quick profits. We're choosing Made in America. We're choosing to believe that American workers, when respected and empowered, can compete with anyone in the world."

The vote was called. One by one, board members voted. Eight for the worker proposal. Three for Blackpave.

The boardroom erupted, Blackpave storming out, Harold following, threatening lawsuits, regulatory complaints, revenge. But their voices were drowned by the cheer from outside as Jennifer, monitoring the meeting by phone, announced the result to the crowd.

Workers embraced, families celebrated, the community cheered. But in the boardroom, the gravity of what had happened was sinking in.

"You understand," Hartwell told John and his team, "this isn't victory. This is responsibility. The ESOP comes with expectations. The improvements must continue. The transformation must sustain."

"It will," Rosa Washington said with quiet confidence. "Because it's not dependent on any individual. It's systemic now. Every worker an improver. Every improvement breeding more improvements. Every success building capability for more success."

Will Moffitt, exhausted from the effort of attending, spoke perhaps his last public words: "Mary Parker Follett said leadership is not the exercise of power but the capacity to increase the sense of power among those led. Today, power increased exponentially. Not because of this vote but because workers proved they could fight for their own value and win."

The celebration in the parking lot continued past sunset. Families picnicked on the grass. Children played in the garden. Workers from three shifts mingled, sharing stories, sharing pride, sharing ownership of their future.

Tommy Kowalski stood with his daughter Angela, watching her interview workers for her documentary.

"Your great-great-grandmother would be proud," he told her. "Anna Kowalski at Hawthorne, being watched but not heard. Now you're ensuring everyone is heard and remembered."

Father Pat offered an impromptu blessing as darkness fell: "The Gospel says the last shall be first and the first shall be last. Today, those who were last, workers, ignored, disrespected, became first. Not through revolution but through revelation, revealing the intelligence that was always there."

David Sterling addressed the crowd as fireworks began over the lake, Syracuse's Fourth of July celebration visible from the parking lot.

"This is Independence Day in more ways than one. Independence from the lie that workers are costs rather than assets. Independence from the tyranny of value extraction. Independence to become what we've always been capable of being."

The fireworks reflected off the windows of Meridian, the old brown brick buildings that had stood for over a century, witness to the rise and fall and rise again of American manufacturing. Inside those buildings, suggestions were becoming improvements, improvements were becoming systems, systems were becoming culture.

Harold Morrison and Richard Blackpave had driven away in separate black cars, defeated but not destroyed. They would try again elsewhere, find other companies to raid, other values to extract. But Meridian was now immune, inoculated by worker ownership, protected by proven value creation.

"What now?" Jennifer Chen asked John as the celebration wound down.

"Now we prove it wasn't a fluke," John said. "We show that this can be sustained, replicated, evolved. We become the model not just for manufacturing but for human organization, proof that power-with creates more value than power-over ever could."

As the last firework faded, workers began cleaning up the parking lot, not because they were told to but because it was their company now, their responsibility, their pride. The transformation that had begun with moving a machine six inches had culminated in moving an entire community.

The boardroom battle was won. But the war, the eternal struggle between those who see workers as costs and those who see them as creators, that war continued.

At Meridian, at least, the creators were winning.

And they would spend the rest of their lives proving they deserved to.

• • •

Will Moffitt's last day at Meridian Manufacturing came on a gray February afternoon, forty-three years to the day after he had first walked through the gates as a young engineer. The factory had changed enormously in those four decades, new buildings, new equipment, new products, but the principles he learned and championed remained constant: respect for workers, value for their wisdom, belief in their capacity to contribute far more than their job descriptions suggested.

John found him in the third-floor office, surrounded by boxes of books that would be donated to the company's new learning center. The photographs on the walls were already packed, but the memories they represented filled the room like invisible presences.

"Nervous about retirement?" John asked.

Will smiled, the expression carrying equal parts satisfaction and uncertainty. "Terrified. I've spent my entire adult life in this building. I have no idea what I'll do with myself when I'm not fighting for worker participation."

"You could write a book. Your experiences would be valuable for others who want to do what we've done here."

"Maybe." Will looked out the window at the factory floor, where workers were moving through their tasks with the purposeful efficiency that had become Meridian's signature. "But the real book is out there. Every worker who thinks about their job instead of just doing it. Every suggestion that turns into an improvement. Every conversation between people who used to see themselves as opponents."

He turned back to John, his expression serious now. "I have one piece of advice for you, and I want you to take it seriously. The transformation we've built here is fragile. It can be sustained, but it can also be destroyed, by neglect, by the wrong leaders, by the gradual accumulation of decisions that prioritize control over collaboration."

"How do I prevent that?"

"You don't prevent it. You can't. Organizations are living things, and living things change in ways that no one can fully control. What you can do is build the capacity for renewal, train leaders who believe in these principles, embed the values so deeply that they become part of how people think, create systems that make deviation from these principles difficult and obvious."

"And if that's not enough?"

Will's smile was sad but accepting. "Then you do your best and accept that some things are beyond your control. Mary Parker Follett worked her entire life for these ideas, and she died without seeing them widely adopted. But her work laid the foundation for everything we've done here. The revolution doesn't have to be completed in any one lifetime. It just has to continue."

They walked together through the factory one last time, Will saying goodbye to workers he had known for decades, John observing the mentor who had shaped his understanding of what management could be. At the gate, Will paused and looked back at the buildings that had been his life's work.

"Take care of them," he said quietly. "The workers, I mean. They trust you with something precious, their belief that this time really is different. Don't let them down."

"I'll try," John said.

"That's all any of us can do." Will extended his hand for a final shake. "The revolution continues, John. Make sure it continues here."

He walked through the gate and didn't look back. John watched until Will's car disappeared down 7th North St, carrying away forty-three years of learning and wisdom, and leaving behind a responsibility that suddenly felt very heavy.

Will died of leukemia shortly thereafter. The revolution would continue. But continuing it would require constant vigilance, constant renewal, constant commitment to principles that most of the business world still rejected. John returned to the factory floor, to the workers who were counting on him, to the work that never ended.

LESSONS LEARNED

The Boardroom as Battleground

Morrison's final assault, the buyout attempt, forced a confrontation between two visions of organizational purpose. One vision sees workers as costs to be minimized. The other vision sees workers as partners to be developed.

Evidence vs. Ideology

The boardroom battle was decided by evidence: documented improvements, verified savings, measurable results. But evidence alone was insufficient; the workers' testimony provided the human dimension that numbers cannot capture. Transformation must be defended with both data and passion.

Creating Value Connection

Creating Value argues that the choice between short-term extraction and long-term creation is not merely ethical but strategic. Companies that prioritize worker engagement build capabilities that compound over time.

CHAPTER 11

The Inheritance Redeemed

"The most valuable 'currency' of any organization is the initiative and creativity of its members. Every leader has the solemn moral responsibility to develop these to the maximum in all his people. This is the leader's highest priority."   — *W. Edwards Deming*

"Top down initiatives fade when consultants leave or leaders change. Sustainable improvement requires embedding problem-solving capability in the workforce itself. "

— Creating Value, (Wiley, 2025)

Winter 1995. The lake had frozen solid enough for ice fishing, and old-timers said it was the coldest winter since 1952; the year Tony Valerio had first proposed his six-inch solution. Inside Meridian, warmth radiated not from the ancient radiators but from something more fundamental: the heat of human energy fully unleashed.

John stood in the memorial garden, now expanded and maintained by workers who'd adopted it as their project. Three new names had been added to the plaque, not deaths but dedications to workers whose ideas had posthumously transformed the company. Tony Valerio's name was among them.

The numbers told one story: revenue up 35% year-over-year, profit margins 14% (industry average: 5%), employee turnover less than 1%, customer satisfaction 99.2%, zero workplace injuries for 200 days, first pass yield ~99%, order backlog six months (customers willing to wait for Meridian quality).

But the human story was richer. John walked through the plant, his daily ritual, though "his" plant was no longer accurate. It belonged to everyone now, and everyone acted like it.

Line 3 hummed with efficiency that looked like ease. Tommy Kowalski had become something between foreman and philosopher, teaching new workers not just tasks but thinking. His station had evolved into a teaching laboratory where visiting manufacturing students from Syracuse University learned that wisdom came from experience, not just education.

"The machine still needs to move another six inches," Tommy said to a group of students with a grin as John approached. "But now I just move it myself. No permission needed. That's the real revolution, not the movement but the permission."

Rosa Washington had been promoted to Vice President of Quality, a title that recognized her actual role.

Her office, by her choice, remained on the factory floor so she could see production while workers could see her, always accessible.

"MIT called," she told John. "They want me to give a keynote lecture on quality at the source. Imagine that a Black woman who was kept as an inspector for twenty years, now teaching MIT engineers."

She smiled, "I said yes, but I'm bringing Tommy and Bobby with me. If they want to learn quality, they need to learn it from all of us."

The transformation had attracted national attention. The Malcolm Baldrige National Quality Award nomination had proceeded to finalist status. But more meaningful was the stream of workers from other plants, other industries, who came to learn not systems but spirit.

"They all ask for our manual," David Sterling said, joining John for the morning walk. "Our business system documentation. As if what we did could be photocopied and applied elsewhere."

"What do you tell them?"

"I tell them we don't have a manual. We have people. And people can't be photocopied."

They passed the suggestion board, not a box anymore but an entire wall, digital and physical combined. Current suggestions, implemented suggestions, and a special section for "Building on History", new ideas that improved on old ones. The implementation rate had stabilized at 82%, with the remaining 18% not rejected but "workshopped" for development.

Jennifer Chen had created a system for tracking improvements.

"Look at this," she showed John on her computer screen. "Three generations of the same family suggesting variations of the same improvement. Grandfather in 1952, father in 1971, son in 1994. Each building on the last, even though the earlier ones were never implemented."

"Inherited wisdom," John mused. "Even suppressed, it survived."

The workshop program had evolved beyond formal sessions. Daily improvements happened spontaneously when problems arose. Cross-functional teams formed and reformed like jazz ensembles, playing different songs with different arrangements but always in harmony.

Father Pat still participated regularly, though his role had evolved from facilitator to what he jokingly called "organizational confessor", the person people told their doubts, their fears, and their hopes.

"The miracle isn't that it worked," he told John during a coffee break. "The miracle is that people still had faith it could work after seventy years of evidence it wouldn't."

The Rapid Response Team, formerly night shift, had become legendary. They'd solved a critical breakdown at a local manufacturer, arriving like a SWAT team of intelligence, diagnosing and fixing a problem their own engineers couldn't solve.

"You saved us three days of downtime," the plant manager had said. "What do we owe you?"

"Nothing," Andre Williams had replied. "But remember this when you're deciding whether to listen to your own workers."

Angela Kowalski's documentary, "Six Inch Moves: The Meridian Story," had premiered at the Syracuse Film Festival and won best documentary. But its real impact was in manufacturing plants across America, where workers showed it to management, saying, "This could be us."

"I get letters," Angela told John. "Workers from Texas, California, Michigan, saying the film gave them hope. Some are even starting their own documentation projects, recording their own ignored intelligence."

The archive of suggestions had become a pilgrimage site for industrial historians. A professor from Cornell had spent three months analyzing patterns, publishing a paper titled "Seventy Years of Suppressed Innovation: The Meridian Archive as American Industrial Tragedy and Triumph."

Bobby Santos had evolved from maintenance supervisor to something unique, Chief Heritage Officer, responsible for preserving and transmitting the accumulated knowledge of generations.

"Every machine tells a story," he said, leading a group of new employees through the plant. "This press here, see the modification? That's from 1987, but it's based on an idea from 1954 that was based on experience from 1923. We're not just running machines. We're running history."

The financial transformation enabled generosity previously impossible.

The worker investment fund had grown to $45 million, with every employee holding shares. Profit-sharing checks averaged $8,000 per worker a quarter, more than some had ever seen at once.

"It's less about the money," Rosa Martinez said, though she admitted the money helped. "It's about investing in something that pays you back. This place has my sweat, my ideas, my improvements. Now I have its profits."

Stefan Pomorski, secure in his role as CFO, had implemented open-book management. Every financial metric was visible to every worker. The mystery and manipulation of numbers had ended.

"Transparency builds trust," he explained to visiting executives. "Trust enables contribution. Contribution creates value. It's not complex, it's circular."

Their friends from Japan wrote: "We came to America in the 1950s to learn. We learned from your workers, your books, your forgotten prophets like Mary Parker Follett, Elton Mayo, Douglas McGregor, Chris Argyris, W. Edwards Deming, and countless other thinkers who understood that organizations are human systems, and that lasting change requires treating people with dignity and respect.

We took that knowledge home and built an industrial miracle. But we always knew the ideas weren't originally ours. Today, we return them to their source, with interest, the interest being recognition that American workers contributed to what the world calls lean management." Tommy accepted the plaque on behalf of all workers, past and present.

"My great-grandmother Anna would have loved this," he said simply. "Not the recognition from others, but the recognition from Meridian. That her intelligence, passed down through generations even when suppressed, finally mattered."

Before Will Moffitt died, he had sent a message, read by Father Pat: "I spent fifty years believing in something I couldn't prove, that workers possessed intelligence that could transform American manufacturing. Today, that belief is fact. But remember: the enemy of transformation isn't resistance but complacency. Keep improving, keep listening, keep proving that power-with creates what power-over never could."

Will's funeral filled St. Brigid's Cathedral, workers and executives, young and old, all mourning a man who'd kept faith in human intelligence when evidence argued against it.

His obituary in the Syracuse Post-Standard read: "William Moffitt, 72, defender of worker dignity, keeper of ignored suggestions, bridge between theory and practice. His legacy lives in every improvement implemented at Meridian and in the principles he championed: that wisdom exists at every level, waiting only for respect to flourish."

Spring brought exciting new challenges. Success had bred interest from larger companies wanting to acquire Meridian, not to destroy it but to replicate it.

• • •

By year-end, the transformation was complete enough to be celebrated but dynamic enough to continue evolving. The Holiday party was held on the factory floor. All three shifts and their families were invited. It was a celebration of collective achievement.

David Sterling spoke briefly: "When I was hired a few years ago, I was told to extract maximum cash and prep for sale. Instead, I've had the privilege of witnessing this renaissance. But I didn't lead this transformation. You did. Workers did. Together. The accumulated intelligence of generations, finally unleashed, did."

But the most moving moment came when Tommy Kowalski unveiled a new addition to the garden, a sculpture commissioned by workers, paid for by their profit-sharing. It was a piece of steel, six inches wide, twisted into a Möbius strip, symbolizing continuous improvement without beginning or end. The plaque read: "In memory of all whose voices went unheard. In honor of all who kept speaking anyway. In celebration of the day listening began. In commitment that it will never stop. **The Six Inch Move That Changed Everything,** January 15, 1993 - Forever"

As snow began to fall on Syracuse, workers and families gathered around the sculpture. Four generations were represented, from Eddie Zawicki's grandson to Catherine Kowalski, in a wheelchair but determined to attend.

"My mother would be so proud," Catherine said, tears freezing on her cheeks. "Anna Kowalski, who they watched at Hawthorne but never really saw. She believed this day would come. It just took seventy years."

John stood with his own family, his wife, his children, his mother who'd finally understood why he'd left Boston for Syracuse.

In his pocket was a letter from his grandmother, given to him that morning:

"Dear John, your grandfather Tony never gave up believing that someday, someone would listen to workers. That someday, intelligence would matter more than authority. He would be so proud that his grandson was part of making that someday today. The six inch move he proposed in 1952 has finally moved, and with it the world. With love and pride, Grandma."

As the party moved inside, out of the cold, John remained in the garden, looking at the sculpture, thinking about cycles and circles, inheritance and redemption.

Mary Parker Follett had written about circular response, ideas building on ideas. W. Edwards Deming had described continuous improvement as a wheel that never stopped turning. The Möbius strip captured both, the endless surface where every point connected to every other point, where ending became beginning, where past became future.

The transformation of Meridian was complete in one sense: the old paradigm was dead, the new one vibrant and self-sustaining. But in another sense, it was just beginning. Every improvement suggested ten more. Every empowered worker empowered others. Every success built capability for greater success.

The six inches had been moved. But six inches, it turned out, was infinite when it kept moving.

As John walked back into the warm plant, where three shifts were celebrating together for the first time in company history, he understood something fundamental: transformation wasn't an event but a state, the state of continuous improvement, choosing to listen with curiosity, of endless recognition that every human being had something to contribute.

The ghost of Frederick Taylor was finally exorcised, replaced by the spirits of Anna Kowalski, Tony Valerio, Miguel Santiago, Rose Santos, and hundreds of others whose intelligence had been suppressed but never destroyed.

Meridian had been redeemed. But more importantly, the principle had been proven when workers are heard, miracles become routine.

Six inch moves at a time.

Forever.

LESSONS LEARNED

The Transition Challenge

Will Moffitt's retirement raises the question every transformation must eventually face: can the principles survive the departure of their champions? The answer depends on whether the transformation has been institutionalized, embedded so deeply in culture and systems that it no longer requires heroic leadership to sustain.

The Continuous Revolution

Deming taught that improvement never ends, that excellence is not a destination but a direction. The Möbius strip sculpture captures this truth: continuous improvement without beginning or end, every point connected to every other point.

Creating Value Connection

In *Creating Value*, Rizzo emphasizes that sustainable transformation requires 'structured emergence,' creating conditions where inclusion and innovation can arise naturally. The revolution continues as long as someone is willing to listen, as long as six-inch moves still matter.

EPILOGUE

The Legacy - Syracuse, 2023

"The most successful leader of all is the one who sees another picture not yet actualized. He sees the things which are not yet there... Above all, he should make his co-workers see that it is not his purpose which is to be achieved, but a common purpose, born of the desires and the activities of the group." — Mary Parker Follett

The morning sun caught the ice crystals on Onondaga Lake, creating a shimmer that seemed to connect past and future. John Valerio, now sixty-seven, walked slowly through the gates of Meridian, his grandson Michael beside him. It was the company's 125th anniversary, and John had been invited back for the celebration, though "back" wasn't quite accurate. He'd never really left, even after retiring five years earlier.

The plant had expanded, not just physically but dimensionally. Where once eight brown brick buildings had stood, now twelve structures created a campus. The newest building, opened in 2020, was called the Anna Kowalski Innovation Center, where workers from companies worldwide came to learn what was now simply called "The Syracuse Way."

"Tell me again about the big move," Michael said. At sixteen, he'd heard the story countless times but never got tired of it. Perhaps because each telling revealed new layers, or perhaps because he understood he was hearing mythology in the making, the origin story of a transformation that had rippled far beyond Syracuse.

"January 15, 1993," John began, but stopped as Tommy Kowalski approached. At seventy-five, Tommy moved with the careful dignity of someone preserving energy for important moments. This was one of them.

"John Valerio," Tommy said, extending a hand that bore the calluses of real work, though he'd been teaching more than doing for the past decade. "And this must be Michael. You have your great-grandfather's eyes."

They walked through the plant, three generations united by story and steel. The factory floor was different now. Robots worked alongside humans, AI systems predicted maintenance needs and programmed machines, digital displays showed real-time metrics. But the fundamental principle of empowerment remained.

"Grandpa Tommy!" A voice called out. Anna Kowalski, yes, another Anna, Tommy's granddaughter, approached in her executive suit. As Chief Operating Officer, she represented the fourth generation of Kowalskis at Meridian, the first to reach senior management.

"We're about to start the ceremony," she said, then smiled at John.

"Mr. Valerio, the workers have something for you." The main floor had been cleared for the celebration. Over a thousand people gathered, current workers, retirees, families, community members. The walls displayed the history: photographs from 1888 to present, the Wall of Remembered Wisdom now digital and interactive, the improvement system that had processed over 100,000 improvements since 1993.

David Sterling, silver haired and sharp as ever, had returned for the anniversary. "When I hired John in 1990," he told the crowd, his voice amplified by speakers, "I thought I was bringing in someone to manage decline. Instead, he helped birth a renaissance."

"We all did," John corrected, but Sterling waved him off.

"Yes, but someone had to listen first. Someone had to move their desk to the floor. Someone had to believe Tommy when he said moving his machine six inches mattered."

The ceremony included presentations of what Meridian had become: 2,400 employees, up from 400 in 1995, $850 million in revenue, 18% profit margins, zero layoffs since 1994, 43 patents filed by floor workers, The Meridian Institute had trained over 1000 workers from dozens of companies, but the numbers were just numbers. The human story was richer.

Stefan Pomorski had passed away in 2018, but his son delivered a message Stefan had recorded for this day: "I spent five years adjusting books to make this company look bad, then twenty-five years showing its real value. The difference? The first served extraction, the second served creation. Never forget: the numbers serve the people, not the opposite."

Rosa Washington appeared on screen via video link from MIT, where at eighty-one she held an honorary degree. "Meridian proved that wisdom doesn't require credentials," she said. "It requires respect. Every company that fails to listen to its workers is leaving gold in the ground."

Bobby Santos's son, Robert Jr., now Chief Heritage Officer, presented the company museum's latest acquisition, the original suggestion box, the one that had been sealed with tape in 1987. "We keep this as a reminder," he said, "of what happens when organizations stop listening. It's our artifact of warning."

A surprise came when Jennifer Chen, now president of an AI company worth millions, announced her gift to Meridian: an endowment of $5 million for the Worker Innovation Fund, providing seed capital for any employee who wanted to start their own business based on their improvements.

"Meridian taught me that creative intelligence exists everywhere," she said via video from Silicon Valley. "This fund ensures that intelligence can flourish anywhere."

Father Pat, ninety-one and moving slowly but still mentally sharp, offered a blessing. Not a religious one but a human one: "In 1993, we moved a machine six inches. But we really moved a mountain, the mountain of disbelief that workers could transform their own work. That mountain had stood for a century. It fell in a day. And it can never be rebuilt because we all remember how to move it."

The formal ceremony gave way to informal celebration. The factory floor became a festival, food trucks run by worker-entrepreneurs, demonstration stations where children could learn manufacturing, the Syracuse Symphony playing (several members were Meridian workers or relatives).

John found himself in the garden, now a small park with benches and the original sculpture at its center. The plaque had been updated annually, adding names of workers whose contributions had been recognized. Tony Valerio's name was near the top, just below Anna Kowalski's.

Michael studied the names. "Did all these people work here?"

"They did more than work here," Tommy said, joining them. "They thought here. They contributed here. They mattered here."

Angela Kowalski, now a successful documentary filmmaker, was filming for a follow-up to her award-winning documentary. She interviewed John and Tommy together, capturing their reflections.

"What surprises you most about how far this has come?" she asked.

"That it took so long to start," Tommy said. "The solutions were always here. My great-grandmother knew at Hawthorne. Your grandfather knew in the 1950s. We just needed someone to say 'yes' instead of 'no'."

"What worries you about the future?" Angela asked John.

"Forgetting," John said after a pause. "Success can breed complacency. New workers who didn't fight for this might take it for granted. New managers might think they know better. The ghost of Frederick Taylor is patient. He's waiting for us to forget that workers are thinkers, not just doers."

As evening approached, the crowd gathered for the lighting of the anniversary display, 125 lights, each representing a year of Meridian history. But the display had been modified by current workers. The first lights were dim, representing the years when worker intelligence was suppressed. The next 30 gradually brightened, showing the transformation. The last 40 blazed brilliantly.

"But look," Anna (the COO) pointed out. "The workers added something." Beyond the 125 historical lights, a string of LEDs stretched into the distance, disappearing around the building, continuing out of sight.

"The future," Anna explained. "Unlimited, as long as we keep listening."

As the celebration wound down, families began departing, but many workers stayed. The second shift was starting. Meridian ran three shifts still, the demand for their products requiring continuous production.

John watched the shift change, remembering his first day in 1990 when workers had barely looked at him. Now they waved, called out greetings, invited him to see their latest improvements.

"Mr. Valerio," a young worker approached, maybe twenty-two, holding a tablet.

"I'm Michael Thompson. I just started last month. I have an idea about the new line, but I wasn't sure if I should suggest it so soon."

Tommy laughed, a sound that filled the space around them. "Son, let me tell you about six inch changes and why every idea matters from day one."

As Tommy told the story again, the machine, the resistance, the movement, the transformation, John realized this was how it survived. Not through documentation or training but through story, passed from worker to worker, generation to generation.

Later, in the executive conference room, now called the Will Moffitt Learning Center, the current leadership team gathered with the old guard. The conversation was about challenges: global competition, automation, climate change, generational differences.

"The principles don't change," Rosa said via video. "Listen, respect, implement, credit. Whether it's a human worker or a human teaching a robot, the principle remains: empower the person closest to the work, they know it best."

COO Anna Kowalski presented the five-year plan. Not a traditional strategic plan but what she called "structured emergence" creating conditions for innovation rather than mandating it.

"We don't know what manufacturing will look like in the future," she admitted. "But we know that workers will figure it out if we let them." As the meeting ended, John stood at the window overlooking the factory floor. The shift was in full swing, the rhythms different from 1993 but the energy the same, humans and machines in collaboration, intelligence flowing in all directions.

Michael joined him. "Do you miss it?"

"Every day," John admitted. "But also, no. Because it doesn't need me anymore. It's self-sustaining." Workers training workers, improvements generating improvements, dignity breeding dignity.

They left through the main entrance, passing under a new addition to the building, words etched in steel above the doors: "Every Worker a Thinker. Every Thinker a Teacher. Every Teacher a Leader. Every Leader a Listener." Below that, smaller but still visible: The Transformation Continues."

As they drove away, John looked back at the illuminated plant, the lights reflecting off the lake, the second shift workers visible through the windows. Some were children of workers he'd known, some were new immigrants bringing fresh perspectives, some were college graduates who chose factory work because at Meridian it meant something more.

"Will it last?" Michael asked.

John thought of Anna Kowalski at Hawthorne, believing her moment of mattering would change everything. Of Tony Valerio, dying bitter but unbroken. Of Tommy Kowalski, carrying three generations of suppressed intelligence. Of Rosa Washington, documenting quality problems for twenty years without recognition. Of Will Moffitt, keeping faith when evidence argued against it.

"It will last as long as people remember that everyone has something to contribute," John said. "As long as six-inch changes still matter. As long as someone is willing to listen."

They drove through Syracuse, past other factories, some thriving using Meridian principles, some struggling with old paradigms, some shuttered and empty. The difference wasn't technology or capital or location. The difference was belief, belief that workers were assets not costs, creators not resources, humans not machines.

At home, John pulled out a worn notebook, his journal from 1993. The entry for January 15 was brief: Moved a machine six inches today. Tommy Kowalski's suggestion. Small movement, big reaction. Something is starting. Don't know what yet, but something.

Below that, he now added: January 15, 2023. Thirty years later. The six inches became miles, the movement became culture, the suggestion became revolution. Tony would be proud. Anna Kowalski would be proud. All the silenced voices would be proud. The revolution not only succeeded, it's continuous.

He closed the journal and thought of tomorrow. Somewhere in Syracuse, in America, in the world, a worker would have an idea. Would anyone listen?

Would the idea be valued? Would the worker matter?

At Meridian, the answer was yes. Had been yes for thirty years. Would be yes for as long as the company existed.

The six-inch movement had become perpetual motion, powered not by physics but by human dignity recognized, human intelligence unleashed, human creativity celebrated.

The ghost of Frederick Taylor was gone.

The spirit of Anna Kowalski lived.

And somewhere a worker was about to suggest a small improvement that would change everything.

Six inch moves at a time.

In hope that every workplace becomes a place where wisdom is welcomed. The revolution is not complete. The revolution is continuous.

The revolution is you.

LESSONS LEARNED

Thirty Years of Sustained Transformation

The epilogue's thirty-year perspective demonstrates that participative management is not a fad but a sustainable approach to organizational excellence. The principles that Mary Parker Follett articulated in the 1920s have proven their durability at Meridian across three decades and multiple generations.

Adaptation Without Abandonment

The transformation survived technological change, generational shifts, competitive pressures, and leadership transitions. This survival required continuous adaptation, applying core principles to changing circumstances while never abandoning the fundamentals.

Creating Value Connection

The epilogue embodies the central argument of *Creating Value*: organizations that treat workers as thinking human beings will outperform organizations that cling to command-and-control approaches. The evidence accumulated at Meridian over thirty years proves that another way of working is possible, practical, and profitable. The revolution continues, six inches at a time, forever.

AFTERWORD

AI and the Future of Empowerment

As I write these final words in 2026, a new revolution is unfolding, one that some fear will render the lessons of this book obsolete. Artificial intelligence, they say, will finally achieve Frederick Taylor's dream: the elimination of human judgment from work, the perfection of process without the messiness of people.

They are wrong. Profoundly, dangerously wrong.

The same voices that dismissed worker intelligence for a century are now dismissing it again, this time in favor of algorithmic intelligence. "AI will do the thinking," they promise. "Workers will simply execute what the machines decide." It is Taylor's ghost in digital form, the same assumption dressed in silicon instead of stopwatches: that wisdom flows only from above, that the people doing the work have nothing to contribute, that efficiency requires the separation of thinking from doing.

But the lesson of Meridian, the lesson of Hawthorne, of Follett, of every transformation documented in these pages, suggests precisely the opposite. AI will not replace worker intelligence. AI will *amplify* it.

Consider what artificial intelligence actually does well: it processes vast amounts of data, identifies patterns invisible to human perception, and generates possibilities at speeds no human can match. What it cannot do is understand context the way a worker standing at a machine understands context. It cannot feel the vibration that signals a bearing about to fail. It cannot read the subtle shift in a colleague's posture that indicates confusion or concern. It cannot know that the theoretical optimum conflicts with the practical reality of a Monday morning after a long weekend.

AI provides information. Workers provide wisdom. The combination is more powerful than either alone.

At the most innovative companies I've studied in recent years, AI is being deployed not to replace worker judgment but to enhance it. Predictive maintenance systems flag potential problems, but experienced workers decide which warnings matter and which are noise. Data analytics reveal patterns in quality defects, but workers who understand the process determine which patterns are actionable. Natural language systems capture and organize improvement suggestions, but the suggestions themselves still flow from human minds engaged with human work.

This is 'power-with' extended to include artificial partners, not 'power-over' implemented through artificial enforcers.

The parallel to Hawthorne is striking. When Elton Mayo's researchers began paying attention to workers, productivity increased regardless of physical conditions. The "Hawthorne Effect" wasn't about lighting or rest breaks; it was about being seen, being valued, being asked. Now imagine that attention amplified: AI systems that listen to every worker, capture every observation, surface every insight that might otherwise be lost. The suggestion box that never closes, the listener that never tires, the memory that never forgets.

Tommy Kowalski waited eighteen months for someone to hear his six-inch suggestion. With AI-enabled systems, that suggestion could be captured instantly, analyzed for impact, connected to similar ideas from other workers, and surfaced for implementation within days. Not because the AI is smarter than Tommy, but because the AI can ensure that Tommy's intelligence reaches the people who need to hear it.

The danger, of course, is real. AI can be deployed in ways that intensify surveillance, accelerate the pace of work beyond human sustainability, and reduce workers to mere appendages of algorithmic systems. In the hands of those who see workers as costs rather than creators, AI becomes just another tool for extraction rather than creation.

But in the hands of those who believe, as I do, as this book argues, that the people doing the work know things that no one else can know, AI becomes something revolutionary: a technology that finally makes it possible to listen to everyone, all the time, and to act on what we hear.

Mary Parker Follett wrote about "circular response," the way ideas build on ideas in groups, creating solutions no individual could imagine alone. She could not have imagined the circles that AI makes possible: global networks of workers sharing insights across time zones and languages, improvement ideas flowing from factory to factory at the speed of light, accumulated wisdom accessible to anyone who needs it.

Elton Mayo discovered that attention transforms performance. AI can provide attention on a scale, not the cold attention of surveillance, but the warm attention of systems designed to value every contribution, surface every insight, and ensure that no voice goes unheard.

W. Edwards Deming taught that quality comes from systems, not heroic individual effort. AI can analyze systems with a comprehensiveness that humans cannot match, identifying the root causes of problems that workers have always sensed but couldn't quite articulate.

The choice before us is the same choice that has always faced organizations: will we use new capabilities to control workers or to empower them? Will AI be deployed as the ultimate time-study man, measuring every motion and punishing every deviation? Or will it be deployed as the ultimate listener, ensuring that worker intelligence finally receives the attention it deserves?

At Meridian, I have no doubt which choice they will make. The culture that was built there; the culture of asking, listening, acting, will embrace AI as a partner in continuous improvement, not a replacement for human judgment. Tommy Kowalski's grandson will use AI tools to capture and share insights that would have taken his great-grandmother Anna months to communicate. Rosa Washington's intellectual heirs will employ machine learning to identify quality patterns that human observation alone could never detect.

And somewhere, a worker will suggest a small improvement that AI analytics flag as potentially significant, an improvement that might have been lost in the old system, buried in a filing cabinet, ignored by managers too busy to listen. But the system will listen. The system will remember. And the improvement will be implemented.

Six inches, amplified by artificial intelligence, becoming six miles.

The revolution continues. The technology changes. The principle remains: the people doing the work already know how to make it better. Our job, with or without AI, is simply to ask, to listen, and to act on what we hear.

Frederick Taylor's ghost will find no home in artificial intelligence, not if we remember that AI, like any tool, reflects the values of those who deploy it. In the hands of those who believe in power-over, AI becomes a weapon of control. In the hands of those who believe in power-with, it becomes an instrument of liberation.

The six-inch move that changed everything at Meridian was never about the physical distance. It was about the dignity of being heard. AI does not threaten that dignity. Properly deployed, it extends that dignity to every worker, in every organization, in every corner of the world.

The workers who taught me everything I know about transformation would not fear artificial intelligence. They would see it for what it is: another tool, waiting to be improved by the people who use it.

They would have suggestions.

And finally, someone, or something, would be ready to listen.

• • •

The future of work is not artificial intelligence versus human intelligence. It is artificial intelligence in service of human intelligence, amplifying the voices that have been silenced for too long, ensuring that the six-inch improvements never stop coming, never stop being heard, never stop changing everything.

Six inch moves at a time.

With AI as our partner in perpetual transformation.

AUTHOR'S NOTE

This novel, while fiction, is grounded in real management theory and practice. The transformation described mirrors hundreds of actual organizational changes documented in management literature.

A note on historical license: The prologue depicting Mary Parker Follett's visit to the Hawthorne Works is fictional dramatization. Will Moffitt is a fictional character intended to honor my mentor, Bill Moffitt.

While Follett's ideas closely paralleled the Hawthorne findings, and her writings from 1927 addressed themes remarkably similar to what Mayo's team would discover, there is no historical record of her visiting the plant. The scene imagines what such an encounter might have revealed, a meeting of complementary insights that, in reality, developed in parallel rather than in conversation.

The theoretical foundations presented are drawn from real management scholarship: Follett's distinction between "power-over" and "power-with"; Mayo's Hawthorne findings about the importance of social factors and attention; McGregor's Theory X and Theory Y assumptions about human motivation; Chris Argyris's work on double-loop learning and organizational defensive routines; and W. Edwards Deming's contributions to continuous improvement and quality management that transformed industry.

The Hawthorne experiments were real, and their findings continue to shape our understanding of human motivation in work settings. The "six-inch move" is inspired by countless similar stories from lean manufacturing implementations, where small changes suggested by workers have produced dramatic improvements that outside experts never anticipated.

The story seeks to make abstract management theory visceral and human, showing how ideas develop through lived experience across generations.

Every theoretical concept is grounded in a human story, because ultimately, organizations are human systems, and transformation happens one relationship, one conversation, one six-inch move at a time.

HISTORICAL APPENDIX

The Intellectual Heritage of Worker Empowerment

The novel traces a continuous thread of management thinking that spans nearly a century, connecting pioneering theorists to contemporary practice. Each thinker built upon predecessors' insights, creating a cumulative body of knowledge about what happens when organizations treat workers as thinking partners rather than interchangeable parts.

Mary Parker Follett (1868–1933) provides the philosophical foundation for the entire narrative. Her distinction between "power-over" (domination) and "power-with" (collaboration) articulates why empowerment works: jointly developed power creates value that coercion cannot. Follett argued that the best solutions emerge through integration, finding approaches that satisfy all parties' genuine interests rather than forcing compromise. Her concept of "circular response," where ideas build upon each other in groups, explains why workshop participants collectively generate insights no individual could achieve alone. Writing in the 1920s, Follett anticipated by decades the participative management principles that would later revolutionize work.

Elton Mayo (1880–1949) and the Hawthorne experiments (1924–1932) demonstrated Follett's theories empirically. When researchers at Western Electric discovered that productivity increased regardless of whether they improved or worsened working conditions, they stumbled upon a profound truth: workers respond to being valued as human beings. The "Hawthorne Effect", the

219

phenomenon of improved performance when people know they are being observed and their opinions matter, revealed that attention, respect, and genuine listening affect productivity more than physical conditions. Mayo's work shifted management thinking from engineering efficiency to understanding human motivation.

Douglas McGregor (1906–1964) crystallized these insights into his famous Theory X and Theory Y framework. Theory X assumes workers are inherently lazy, require control, and avoid responsibility. Theory Y assumes workers are self-motivated, seek responsibility, and want to contribute meaningfully. McGregor argued that management assumptions become self-fulfilling prophecies: treat workers as untrustworthy and they behave accordingly; treat them as capable partners and they rise to the expectation. His work at MIT influenced a generation of managers.

Chris Argyris (1923–2013) explained why organizations resist the very changes they claim to want. His concept of "double-loop learning" distinguishes between fixing problems within existing assumptions versus questioning the assumptions themselves. Argyris identified "organizational defensive routines," the unconscious patterns that protect individuals from embarrassment while preventing genuine learning. His work illuminates why Morrison and other resisters in the novel cling to control-based management even as evidence mounts against it.

W. Edwards Deming (1900–1993) translated these human-centered insights into systematic practice. His philosophy of continuous improvement, refined in post-war Japan and returned to America as part of the "Japanese miracle," emphasized that quality comes from empowering workers to identify and solve problems at the source. Deming taught that most performance problems stem from systems, not individuals, and that sustainable improvement requires embedding problem-solving capability throughout the workforce. His famous fourteen points for management remain a blueprint for organizational transformation.

The Journey

These thinkers share a fundamental conviction: workers possess intelligence, creativity, and knowledge that most organizations systematically ignore. The tragedy dramatized in *Nobody Ever Asked Before* is not that this wisdom doesn't exist, it's that generation after generation of workers have waited for someone to ask.

The novel argues that empowerment is not soft-headed idealism but hard-headed strategy. Organizations that tap worker intelligence consistently outperform those that don't, not despite their focus on human dignity but because of it. The "six-inch move" represents this truth made tangible: a small adjustment suggested by a worker who understood his job better than any outside expert could, producing results that years of top-down initiatives never achieved.

From Follett's philosophical framework through Mayo's empirical discoveries, McGregor's psychological insights, Argyris's understanding of resistance, and Deming's systematic methodology, these thinkers constructed an intellectual tradition that the novel brings to life through story, character, and the accumulated wisdom of workers finally being heard.

BIBLIOGRAPHY

Argyris, Chris. *Overcoming Organizational Defenses: Facilitating Organizational Learning.* Boston: Allyn and Bacon, 1990.

Argyris, Chris. *Reasoning, Learning, and Action: Individual and Organizational.* San Francisco: Jossey-Bass, 1982.

Byrne, Art, with James P. Womack. *The Lean Turnaround: How Business Leaders Use Lean Principles to Create Value and Transform Their Company.* New York: McGraw-Hill, 2012.

Deming, W. Edwards. *Out of the Crisis.* Cambridge, MA: MIT Press, 1986.

Drucker, Peter F. *The Practice of Management.* New York: Harper & Row, 1954.

Follett, Mary Parker. *Creative Experience.* New York: Longmans, Green and Co., 1924.

Follett, Mary Parker. *Dynamic Administration: The Collected Papers of Mary Parker Follett.* Edited by Henry C. Metcalf and L. Urwick. New York: Harper & Brothers, 1942.

Mayo, Elton. *The Human Problems of an Industrial Civilization.* New York: Macmillan, 1933.

McGregor, Douglas. *The Human Side of Enterprise.* New York: McGraw-Hill, 1960.

Ohno, Taiichi. *Toyota Production System: Beyond Large-Scale Production.* Portland, OR: Productivity Press, 1988.

Rizzo, John. *Creating Value: Empowering People for Sustainable Success.* (Wiley, 2025).

Roethlisberger, Fritz J., and William J. Dickson. *Management and the Worker: An Account of a Research Program Conducted by the Western Electric Company, Hawthorne Works, Chicago.* Cambridge, MA: Harvard University Press, 1939.

Taylor, Frederick Winslow. *The Principles of Scientific Management.* New York: Harper & Brothers, 1911.

ABOUT THE AUTHOR

John Rizzo is a leader at Talus Holdings and MoffittXL. With over thirty years of experience leading transformational changes across many organizations, he has facilitated over one thousand team improvement workshops.

His philosophy of "value creation" versus "value extraction" has helped companies achieve dramatic improvements, including enterprise value increases in the hundreds of percent.

The stories in this novel are fictional but grounded in real experiences. The "six-inch move" is based on actual events when a worker's simple suggestion changed everything he believed about management.

Rizzo is also the author of *Creating Value: Empowering People for Sustainable Success That Benefits Employees, Customers, and Owners* (Wiley, 2025).

John is always willing to discuss creating value at johnarizzo1@icloud.com.